The Question of Dependency and Economic Development

The Question of Dependency and Economic Development

A Quantitative Analysis

Brian R. Farmer

LEXINGTON BOOKS
Lanham • Boulder • New York • Oxford

LEXINGTON BOOKS

Published in the United States of America
by Lexington Books
4720 Boston Way, Lanham, Maryland 20706

12 Hid's Copse Road
Cumnor Hill, Oxford OX2 9JJ, England

British Library Cataloguing in Publication Information Available

Library of Congress Cataloging-in-Publication Data

Farmer, Brian R., 1959–
    The question of dependency and economic development : a
quantitative analysis / Brian R. Farmer.
        p. cm.
    Includes bibliographical references and index.
    ISBN 0-7391-0025-4 (cl. : alk. paper)
    1. Developing countries—Dependency on foreign countries.
    2. Developing countries—Economic policy. 3. Economic development.
    I.   Title.
    HC59.7.F344 1999
    337'.09172'4—dc21

Printed in the United States of America

∞™ The paper used in this publication meets the minimum requirements of American
National Standard for Information Sciences—Permanence of Paper for Printed Library
Materials, ANSI/NISO Z39.48–1992.

To Denise, Glen, and Janet, who have provided the support that made this possible, and to Bob, whose quantitative wizardry will never be forgotten.

Contents

List of Tables   xi

1. Introduction: Scope and Purpose   1

2. Development and Dependency Literature   7

     Modernization Theory and the Liberal Paradigm   7

     Dependency Origins   11

     Radical Dependency Literature   14

     New Dependency   19

     General Consensus   23

     Disagreements   25

3. Measurement and Empirical Studies   29

     Measuring Dependency   29

     Empirical Studies   33

     Dependency and Economic Growth   33

     Dependency and Inequality   36

     Other Empirical Studies   40

4. Methods and Data   43

     Hypotheses   43

     Independent Variables: Dependency   46

     Dependent Variables   54

     Control Variables   59

Data   64

Multicolinearity, Heteroskedasticity, and Autoregression   65

Overview of Operations   66

5. Factor and Bivariate Analyses   71

The Sample   71

Dependency: One-Dimensional or Multidimensional?   72

Bivariate Analysis   73

Bivariate Relationships: Independent Variables   74

Bivariate Relationships: Dependency and Control Variables   76

Bivariate Relationships: Control, and Dependent Variables   77

Dependency and GNP per Capita   79

Dependency and Growth   81

Dependency and Inequality   82

Dependency and PQLI   84

Dependency and Quality Improvement   86

Summary: Bivariate Analysis   88

6. Dependency, Wealth, and Growth   89

Data Analysis: GNP per Capita   90

Pooled Regressions: GNP per Capita   91

Pooled Regressions with Controls: GNP per Capita   92

Data Analysis: Economic Growth   94

Pooled Regressions: Economic Growth   95

Pooled Regression with Controls: Economic Growth   97

7. Dependency and Inequality   103

Data Analysis: Inequality   103

Pooled Regression: Inequality   !04

Pooled Regression: Inequality with Controls   105

Dependency and Growth of Inequality   108

8. Dependency and PQLI   109

Data Analysis: PQLI 109

Pooled Regression: PQLI 110

Pooled Regression with Controls: PQLI 112

Data Analysis: Quality Improvement 115

Pooled Regression: Quality Improvement 116

Pooled Regression: Quality Improvement with Controls 117

9. Summary and Conclusions 121

Appendices

A. The Sample 127

B. GLS Diagnostics 129

Select Bibliography 131

Index 139

About the Author 151

Tables

4.1	Operationalization: Dependency and GNP per Capita	66
4.2	Operationalization: Dependency and Growth	66
4.3	Operationalization: Dependency and Inequality	67
4.4	Operationalization: Dependency and PQLI	67
4.5	Operationalization: Dependency and Quality Improvement	67
5.1	Rotated Factor Matrix	73
5.2	Correlation Matrix: Independent Variables	75
5.3	Correlations: Dependency and Control Variables	76
5.4	Composite Correlation Matrix	78
5.5	Bivariate Relationships: GNP per Capita	79
5.6	Bivariate Relationships: GNP per Capita Growth	81
5.7	Bivariate Relationships: Inequality	83
5.8	Bivariate Relationships: Dependency and PQLI	84
5.9	Bivariate Relationships: Quality Improvement	87
6.1	GNP per Capita Statistics	91
6.2	Dependency and GNP per Capita: No Controls	91
6.3	Dependency and GNP per Capita	93
6.4	GNP per Capita Growth Statistics	95
6.5	Dependency and Growth: No Controls	96
6.6	Dependency and Growth with Controls	97
7.1	Inequality Statistics	103
7.2	Dependency and Inequality: No Controls	104

7.3	Dependency and Inequality with Controls	106
8.1	Physical Quality of Life Index	109
8.2	Dependency and PQLI: No Controls	110
8.3	Dependency and PQLI with Controls	113
8.4	Quality Improvement Statistics	116
8.5	Dependency and Quality Improvement: No Controls	117
8.6	Dependency and Quality Improvement with Controls	118
9.1	Composite of Analysis	123
B.1	Residual Variance Ratios	137

Chapter 1

Introduction: Scope and Purpose

The subject of development (or underdevelopment) has become, since the 1960's, one of the dominant subjects of inquiry in comparative politics. Hard evidence to support this fact can be found in the seemingly endless stream of social science research probing the phenomena of development and underdevelopment (Almond, 1987, p. 437). The emphasis on development suggests that the problems of development and underdevelopment in the current international polity are among the preeminent, if not the most important, political problems in the post cold war era.

During the post-war era, developing countries were offered a choice between two competing paradigms of development, one capitalist and one socialist. Since the collapse of the Soviet Union and the Communist bloc and the marketization of the People's Republic of China, developing countries are experiencing a narrowing of the field of development choices to the ones espoused by the cold war victors: marketization of their economies, democratization of their polities, and integration with the international capitalist political economy.

The North American Free Trade Agreement (NAFTA) and the current round of the General Agreement on Trade and Tariffs (GATT) exemplify the development choice toward which most lesser developed countries (LDCs) appear to be moving. Samuel Huntington (1991), for example, documents a recent "third wave" of democratization that has accompanied the recent marketization. This development path is essentially classic liberal in character and has been labeled by political scientists as the "modernization perspective" (So, 1990, p. 17).

This movement of LDCs toward democracy and marketization is occurring despite a large body of scholarly literature, labeled as the "dependency" perspective, which holds that LDCs should view such marketization and integration with a great deal of trepidation. The dependency perspective is a critique of, and an alternative explanation to, the dominant liberal modernization paradigm that has provided the theoretical foundation for the postwar international political-economic order. This competing paradigm, essentially Marxist-Leninist in character, until recently enjoyed a healthy following both among scholars and statesmen in LDCs. With the collapse of the communist bloc and subsequent discreditation of Marxist-Leninist economic perspectives, the dependency perspective appears to have fallen out of fashion among both scholars and policy makers. We argue that a paradigm should not be discarded merely because it is now out of fashion, but only when it is no longer useful due

1

to its failure to accurately describe, explain, and predict political phenomena. The dependency perspective has not yet been subjected to the sufficient, comprehensive, longitudinal, empirical analysis necessary to merit its discard. The purpose of this study is to assess the merits of the dependency perspective by testing the dependency argument through indicators derived from dependency literature.

The basic argument of the dependency perspective is that a political-economic condition labeled as "dependency" produces "underdevelopment" in LDCs. The dependency perspective itself is not monolithic, and underdevelopment is a multifaceted concept that encompasses different phenomena depending on which segment of the dependency perspective one espouses. Underdevelopment in dependency literature typically includes low GNP per capita, low rates of GNP per capita growth, high rates of inequality in income distribution, bureaucratic authoritarian political regime types, and a failure of the political-economic system in meeting the basic human needs of the masses. This research then will investigate the relationship between dependency and each of these phenomena.

There have been numerous attempts at empirical analysis of the dependency perspective as we will present later; however, we argue that scholarship on the effects of dependency is insufficient and that dependency is in need of further empirical research. More specifically, we argue that the current literature regarding the relationships between dependency and growth, equality, and the quality of life in lesser developed countries (LDCs) remains incomplete.

The incompleteness of empirical studies in dependency is captured well by Volker Bornschier et al. (1978). This survey of empirical literature reveals that previous studies (see, for example, Rubinson, 1976; Stoneman, 1975) have often been cross-sectional, but not longitudinal; therefore, they can capture neither the long-term effects nor the causal relationships of dependency on development. Conversely, other studies (Stevenson, 1972; Stoneman, 1975; Papanek, 1973) are longitudinal, yet offer empirical analysis merely on elements of dependency such as penetration by multinational corporations rather than the concept of dependency itself. Additionally, many studies (see, for example, Griffin and Enos, 1970; Kaufman et al., 1975; Stevenson, 1972; Szymanski; 1976) include no control variables for factors that may confound the relationships between dependency and other phenomena, such as growth and inequality. Without the relevant control variables, scholars cannot eliminate the possibility that anemic economic growth or inequality in LDCs may be due in part to internal factors such as regime type, small area, population growth, or small population size (Bornschier, 1978).

A large number of other studies (see, for example, Alschuler, 1976; Evans, 1972; Griffin and Enos, 1970; Kaufman et al., 1975; Stevenson, 1972; Szymanski, 1976; McGowan and Smith, 1978) focus on a particular geographic area, such as Latin America or Africa, instead of incorporating a multi-regional, cross-national focus and, therefore, are unable to eliminate the possibility that the effects of dependency are geographically specific. Although many of these studies are meritorious, the dependency paradigm yet, at least in an empirical sense, remains incomplete. Under the dependency framework, dependency is thought to impact development in all LDCs, not just those in any given geographic area. Moreover, dependency is widely recognized to be a multifaceted concept that is not captured by a single indicator. Therefore, studies that focus on only one indicator of dependency, such as direct foreign investment, are rendered insufficient as analyses of dependency. Additionally, the effects of dependency are said to be long term and continuous and, therefore, cannot be properly captured cross-sectionally. Hence, this research is necessary to improve upon the works of previous scholars by implementing a longitudinal cross-national design where dependency is represented as a multifaceted concept.

The goals of this research, however, go beyond merely fine-tuning the empirical analyses of previous scholars. A major goal of this research is to investigate the relationship between the multifaceted concept of dependency and the physical quality of life in LDCs. This goal is driven by the argument of dependency theorists that dependency produces inequality and is therefore undesirable, an argument that ignores the possibility that lower segments of societies in LDCs may experience improved conditions with dependency despite any such increases in inequality. Hence, the negative effects (in a normative sense) of any increase in inequality produced by dependency may be lessened if physical quality of life tends to increase with dependency.

We argue in both a normative and a non-normative sense that a major goal of development strategies is that of meeting basic human needs and that meeting basic human needs is, arguably, at least as important a development goal as growth or reducing inequities. If, indeed, dependency is positively related to inequality, as claimed by Cardoso and Faletto (1979) and even if dependency theorists are correct in the assertion that dependency mainly benefits the upper classes (Cardoso, 1973), then the increase in income gap may be due to a more rapid increase in the living standard of the upper classes relative to those of the lower classes and have no detrimental effect on the quality of life or living standard of the lower classes in LDCs. In fact, it is possible that quality of life in LDCs in this sense could rise simultaneously with growth and inequality.

Consequently, we intend to fill this void in the literature by investigating the relationship between dependency and quality of life in LDCs. Results from the dependency/quality of life relationship should be useful in determining whether any inequality produced by dependency in LDCs, if it is indeed produced at all, is as detrimental to the lower classes in LDCs as dependency theorists suggest.

Still another weakness in the dependency argument, as well as in previous empirical studies of dependency relationships, is the omission of the possibility that income inequality in LDCs has a stronger relationship with growth than with dependency. The omission of the possibility that inequality in LDCs has a stronger relationship with growth than with dependency is essentially due to a lack of sufficient control variables and is, in this respect, merely a portion of a larger methodological problem which has thus far plagued dependency research. In a survey of the empirical studies investigating the relationship between MNC penetration and inequality, Bornschier et al. (1978) find the preponderance of work to support the dependency contention that dependency is positively related to inequality. Although we applaud the efforts and contributions of these empirical studies and their findings, we argue that tests of the relationship between MNC penetration and inequality are not tests of dependency, but merely one facet of dependency and are, therefore, insufficient to conclude that dependency produces inequality. Furthermore, in all the empirical studies investigating the MNC penetration/inequality relationship reviewed by Bornschier et al. (1978), scholars failed to control for growth, and it is with this omission that we take issue.   Growth has been hypothesized by a number of scholars including Samuel Huntington and Joan Nelson (1976), Simon Kuznets (1955), and Mancur Olson (1963), to be related in one form or another to equality. Consequently, the relationship which scholars have observed between foreign investment and inequality may be confounded by economic growth. We will then improve upon the works of previous scholars by implementing controls for growth in the analysis.

    If the inequality in LDCs is primarily a product of growth, then one should expect quality of life indicators in LDCs to improve simultaneously with inequality; consequently, we argue that the detrimental effect of inequality in LDCs may be minimized if quality of life indicators tend to enjoy a positive relationship with inequality. Hence, the associated dependent development argument of Fernando Cardoso (1973, pp. 171-172) and Cardoso and Enzo Faletto (1979, p. xxv) that there may be growth in dependent economies, but that dependent growth produces inequality and depresses quality of life, loses some of its attractiveness if quality of life indicators improve simultaneously with the dependent growth. Improvement in quality of life indicators suggests that the poorest segments of the populations in LDCs do not suffer ill effects from increases in inequality, if indeed there are any increases in inequality, in an absolute sense, but instead have only become worse off than their fellow countrymen in a relative sense. For these reasons, we will investigate the relationship between dependency and quality of life in LDCs, along with the impact of dependency on growth and inequality.

    In the investigation of the relationship between dependency and the physical quality of life (PQLI) in LDCs, it is possible that dependency may prove to be associated with lower PQLI, but not be a factor which perpetuates low PQLI. In other words, an observed association between dependency and low PQLI may very well be spurious, similar to the association between individual height and the height of siblings. Clearly, there is a tendency among tall persons to have tall siblings, but the association is not causal and the reason for the relationship can be discovered elsewhere. To establish the direction of the causal arrow in the dependency/PQLI relationship, it is necessary to investigate the relationship between dependency and the growth or improvement of PQLI (Quality Improvement). If dependency proves to be associated with slower Quality Improvement, then the logical conclusion is that dependency is a phenomenon which perpetuates the lower PQLI with which it is associated. If dependency is not related to slower Quality Improvement, then the reverse is logically correct, and dependency does not perpetuate or cause lower PQLI, but should then be viewed merely as a characteristic of states with lower PQLI; the causes of which are to be found elsewhere.

As will be shown in this study, another omission in the empirical studies of dependency/inequality relationships is the failure to control for regime type. Abbas Pourgerami's (1991) empirical results suggest that democracy enjoys a complementary relationship with economic and political freedom, and, conversely, authoritarian regimes are more likely to "lead to situations in which some elite units enjoy progress and modernity, while the majority remain socio-economically impoverished and politically repressed" (Pourgerami, 1991, p. 136). In other words, inequality and PQLI in LDCs may be related to the internal factor of regime type as opposed to external dependency factors. Consequently, one would expect inequality to be less severe in democracies due to the ability of citizens to make demands on government, an ability which may exist to a lesser degree in authoritarian states.

For their part, dependency theorists (Cardoso and Faletto, 1979, p. 153) argue that growth in dependent states is not possible without authoritarian regimes due to the need to control the political unrest, which stems from inequalities produced by dependency. Clearly, regime type may be an important factor in explaining growth, inequality, and physical quality of life in LDCs. Therefore, we will attempt to improve on the works of previous scholars by including controls for regime type in the analysis of the dependency/growth and dependency/equity relationships, as well as the relationship between dependency and quality of life in LDCs.

Our purpose is to provide an empirical test of the relationship between dependency and economic development in LDCs, as represented by GNP per capita, GNP per capita growth, inequality, PQLI and Quality Improvement. Analysis will be conducted cross-nationally and longitudinally on as many cases for which data are available and adequate. Dependency, as suggested by dependency literature, will be represented as a multifaceted concept with variables selected based upon their consistency with the dependency framework. Controls will be introduced to reduce the possibility that the relationships discovered are indeed spurious or internally caused. Essentially, we hope to provide empirical support for the arguments that growth increases with dependency, inequality is unrelated to dependency, and quality of life increases with dependency.

The importance of this research is underlined by the current marketization and capitalist integration policies of many LDCs and international lending institutions. If dependency theorists are correct, the current policies being pursued globally may have disastrous consequences for growth and income equality in LDCs. Dependency theorists argue that the integration of LDCs into the world economy will be asymmetric in character and will produce underdevelopment in LDCs as well as structural problems in local economies and polities which will produce inequality (Jackson, 1979, p. 44). Although it is common for governments to implement policies before their implications have been thoroughly tested by social scientists, because these policies are pursued without adequate empirical analysis of the relationship between dependency and development, the ramifications are in some respects frightening. This research is an attempt to provide empirical evidence which either supports or rejects the current marketization strategies and, therefore, serve either as an endorsement for these policies or as fair warning.

There is another motive which drives this research. Over the last three decades, there has perhaps been no idea that has stirred more lively debate in comparative politics than the dependency perspective. The dependency perspective garnered a host of articulate adherents as well as detractors, and the debates over its merits occupied a substantial amount of space in professional journals. Although the "modernization" perspective appears at present to have become the dominant paradigm and dependency currently appears to be passé, dependency once commanded a tremendous amount of space in development literature. The sheer volume of dependency literature demands that it should not be buried without adequate testing. In sum, we hope that the findings here will be significantly supportive or unsupportive of the dependency arguments and, thereby, able to act as confirmation of current Third World development strategies or sound an alarm for the policymakers who have joined the free market bandwagon without sufficient empirical investigation of the arguments of dependency theorists.

We will begin this study with a survey of the development and dependency literature followed by an overview of previous empirical studies that centered on dependency. We will then proceed to introduce the methodology for the empirical analysis of our own, followed by the presentation of data and analysis. Finally, conclusions will be drawn from the data analysis, providing new understanding of the relationship between dependency and economic development.

Chapter 2

Development and Dependency Literature

Below, a brief review of the dominant liberal development paradigm, the modernization perspective, which dependency theory contradicts, is sketched to illuminate the conflict of the dependency theory with the dominant paradigm. A brief account of the origins and history of the dependency school of thought follows, as well as a brief literature review of the dependency perspective. Included is a survey of previous empirical analysis of dependency and a review of the literature surrounding physical quality of life in LDCs.

Modernization Theory and the Liberal Paradigm

The liberal paradigm is perhaps the most prevalent perspective on political economy and has remained so in one form or another since its original formulation (Ellsworth, 1969, p. 23). Major points of emphasis of the liberal paradigm include laissez-faire capitalism, limited government, and Social Darwinism. The underlying basic assumption of the liberal paradigm is that perfect competition and an unfettered market would produce maximum economic growth and development. Free trade in the international realm and free movement of capital are viewed as forces that would maximize world production through optimal efficiency in resource allocation. Maldistribution of goods, either within or among states, is assumed to be nonproblematic under the liberal paradigm. In the words of D.A. Snider (1971, p. 426), "The presumption is strong that an expansion in any part of the economy tends to have favorable effects on the other parts." Furthermore, free market forces would tend to work toward equalization of both prices and incomes in both the domestic and international realms (Cline, 1975, p. 372). The basic argument is that trade and foreign capital, whether in the form of direct investment, aid, or loans, are inversely related to inequality in income distribution. In the words of W.R. Cline (1975, p. 372):

> Under normal neoclassical assumptions, foreign investment must equalize rather than concentrate domestic income, even if it uses more capital intensive techniques than domestic investment. Foreign investment must raise labor's share in the national income by: (a) creating more jobs; and (b) reducing the marginal product of capital (and hence its price) and raising that of labor (and hence wages).

Under the liberal paradigm, where maldistribution does occur, its causes are assumed to be related to forces that violate free market principles rather than to

7

the free market itself (Ellsworth, 1969). In short, under the liberal paradigm, trade, foreign investment, and aid are viewed as inversely related to income inequality.

The liberal paradigm has its ideological base in the works of Adam Smith (1776). Smith argued for the removal of the state from economic decisions and the reliance on a self-regulating free market. Smith's laissez-faire policies included political liberalism, free trade, hard currency based on the gold standard, balanced budgets, and minimal income redistribution to the lower classes. Smith argued that private profit and public welfare would become reconciled through impersonal forces of market competition.

According to the liberal paradigm, trade plays a major role in producing growth in underdeveloped economies. As explained by Snider (1971) and Cline (1975), the classical view is that LDCs should export those goods for which they enjoy a "comparative advantage," and import those goods for which they do not hold a comparative advantage. Essentially, a comparative advantage is held by a state if it is able to produce a particular product at less cost than its trading partner. Through this trade the economy becomes more efficient since it focuses only on the things that it is able to do well and simply trades for products it is unable to produce efficiently. The increased efficiency in turn should produce a rise in exports for LDCs, and therefore a rise in income, which in turn can be used to further new investment opportunities in other sectors and purchase a greater volume of consumer goods thereby increasing the standard of living of the populace. The coinciding rise in imports purchased with the growing wealth from exports also brings with it the added benefit of imported technology, broadening both skills and knowledge and leading again to greater efficiency. In the liberal view, as argued by Michael Dolan and Brian Tomlin (1980, p. 45), trade is an "engine of growth."

According to the liberal paradigm, another factor which is vital to growth in LDCs is investment (Snider, 1971). Capital for investment may be in the form of direct foreign investment, aid, or loans. Aid under the liberal paradigm should have the greatest impact on economic growth since, unlike direct foreign investment or loans, there are no repayments nor are there servicing charges. Snider (1971, p. 441) argues that foreign capital leads to increased net productivity, enlarged employment opportunities, higher wages, and increased government tax revenues. Finally, as with trade, capital transfers, whether they are in the form of aid, direct foreign investment, or loans, also tend to play a role in the beneficial transfer of technology to LDCs (Snider, 1971). In sum, foreign capital for investment, whether in the form of aid, loans, or direct foreign investment, should increase consumer demand as a result of higher income and produce a higher level of technology and technical skill among the populace, in turn producing economic growth.

The liberal paradigm has perhaps never been implemented in its purest form; however, the basic principles of the liberal paradigm were credited with the growth and modernization of the industrialized nations of Europe and the

Western Hemisphere during the 19th century (Dillard, 1992). This growth and industrialization of the U.S. and European nations under the liberal paradigm of the 19th century is undeniable; however, equally undeniable is the fact that the industrialized states also experienced large income gaps and poverty among the lower classes (Dillard, 1992).

Due to the plight of the lower classes, critics of the liberal paradigm, such as Karl Marx, appeared and gained influence (Moran, 1978). After World War I, the industrialized nations were, in the majority, unable to return to the prosperity and growth of the 19th century and many of the tenets of the liberal paradigm were abandoned. Protectionist trade barriers were erected almost universally during the 1930's as were balanced budgets. Governments became much more involved in income redistribution and insuring employment, and the hard currency standard was abandoned (Dillard, 1992).

By the 1930's, the liberal paradigm had undergone a seemingly irreversible transformation in practice which accepted and embraced the arguments of John Maynard Keynes (1936), that it was legitimate for the state to interfere in the market to promote stable growth and to correct the imbalances and dislocation produced by the imperfections in the market (Dillard, 1992). Interestingly, when scholars of political economy turned their attention to the underdeveloped world after WWII, there was a tendency to return to the nineteenth century liberal paradigm, which had failed the developed world in the twentieth century and apply it to developing countries as a guide for development. This classic liberal paradigm then became the basis for the modernization paradigm of development which was the dominant paradigm of development in the post WWII era.

The modernization perspective, influenced by the evolutionary ideas of Charles Darwin and Herbert Spencer as well as the liberal economic ideas of Adam Smith, was the dominant development paradigm prior to the emergence of the dependency perspective in the 1960's. The basic tenet is that societies, similar to individuals, evolve through stages of growth or development directionally from undeveloped to developed. Hence, western industrialized nations tend to be viewed by modernization theorists as "developed" while states in the Third World are labeled as undeveloped. Modernization theorists suggest that LDCs should try to emulate western industrialized nations if they desire to achieve growth and development. For modernization theorists, it is assumed that growth and development are both desirable and good for LDCs.

The modernization perspective is a liberal theory derived from the experience of western industrialized nations where traditional, agricultural societies were slowly transformed into the modern industrialized states of the present. The laissez-faire capitalist economic system is credited with being a major contributor to the development of the industrialized west, allowing both states and individuals to be more productive in pursuit of their own interests and subsequently producing development. On the basis of the experiences of these western industrialized states, development is purported by modernization scholars to be a unidirectional, evolutionary process whereby states develop harmoniously in terms of their social, political, and economic realms. All aspects of society tend to develop together and all aspects of society benefit (So, 1990, p. 20; Apter, 1990).

David Apter (1990) labels this body of literature as "Modernization I." According to Apter, Modernization I theorists view development as the eradication of traditional elements in society, replacing them with western institutions and norms. The perspective is integrative in character, with the bulk of development forces viewed as positive, and naturally occurring together. Increased participation, democracy, and integration are all expected components along with the accompanying expansion of choice.

Typifying this view is the work of S.M. Lipset (1963). Lipset argues that the least common denominator which links political systems to other components of the society is that "democracy is related to the state of economic development" (1963, p. 31). "The more well-to-do a nation, the greater the chances it will sustain democracy." Also typifying the modernization perspective is the work of W.W. Rostow (1964). Rostow offered a central tenet to the modernization perspective, arguing that development occurs in stages. Rostow asserts that nations begin as traditional, agricultural societies, then progress through a precondition state where industries and markets begin to develop. In order for states to develop past this stage, Rostow prescribes that investment must be increased in production. Rostow argues that population growth hinders this "takeoff." Hence, the major impediments and impetus to development are internal in nature, rather than external. Rostow argues that the largest impediment to growth in LDCs is lack of capital for investment in production; consequently, he prescribes increased aid from industrialized states for the purpose of investing in production.

Similar to Rostow, Marion Levy (1967) argues that development consists of a continuum between modernized and unmodernized societies. Levy also contends that all societies will eventually develop until they resemble the modern industrialized nations. Levy (1967, pp. 196-201) also asserts that LDCs in the late twentieth century are at an advantage because they can learn from the patterns established from the already developed states and are able to borrow their expertise. Also in concurrence with Rostow's stage development thesis, James Coleman (1968) identifies different stages or "crises" of development which emerge from the modernization process. Developing countries must pass through each stage or crisis in order to achieve the successes of the western industrialized states.

Another thread which ties these modernization scholars together is the view which regards obstructions to development as internal. Neil Smelser (1964) argues that development is stunted in LDCs due to a lack of the resources, both human and physical, that are necessary to create modern institutions which are capable of coordinating activities. Similarly, Lucian Pye (1966) argues that an integrative system of mass communication, which is often lacking in LDCs, is necessary for development. In either case, Smelser and Pye view underdevelopment as an internal problem related to structural obstructions to development.

In addition to these structural impediments to development, Smelser and others, such as Gabriel Almond and Sydney Verba (1963), contend that underdevelopment may stem from cultural impediments to development. Smelser (1964) argues that the traditional values and traditional political structures found in LDCs are impediments to development. Almond and Verba (1963) stress the value of a "civic culture" in which social values favorable to democracy are present as a prerequisite for development. The inference is that LDCs did not develop due to their cultures which acted as internal impediments to development. Daniel Lerner (1958) argued that development required the development of "modern personalities" among individuals in LDCs who embraced science, democracy, and free market capitalism.

In sum, modernization theorists posit that LDCs have failed to develop because they have veered from the evolutionary path of the industrialized West. The major impediments to adopting the proper evolutionary path are domestic in character. Though development in LDCs is eventually inevitable, it has been impeded by traditional structures within LDCs, hindering the adoption of the proper development path. Contact with industrialized nations is desirable for LDCs in order to learn the proper path to development through the example, aid, trade, and technology sharing of the industrialized states. It is this classic liberal modernization paradigm from which the dependency perspective arose as a reaction after WWII.

Dependency Origins

Discussed in the following section are the works of the major early contributors leading to the construction of the theory of dependency. This review includes focuses on the contributions of Albert Hirschman (1945), Raul Prebisch (1950, 1961, 1964), and Gunnar Myrdal before the rapid expansion of dependency literature following the publication of Andre Gunder Frank's (1967) seminal work.

The dependency perspective itself is grounded in the Marxist and Leninist perspectives on imperialism. The notion that powerful capitalist nations would use trade and the capitalist system to exploit other nations for their own gain is clearly present in the writings of both Marx and Lenin; however, it should be noted that there are some important differences between dependency and the writings of Marx and Lenin on imperialism. First, Marx and Lenin were concerned with explaining the causes of imperialism originating from contradictions in capitalism. Dependency theorists are instead primarily interested in the consequences of imperialist relations for LDCs. Hence, although the arguments of Marx and Lenin as to the causes of imperialism are not of critical significance to dependency theory, they are important in substantiating the argument that it is the association with capitalism that produces the dependent economies in LDCs in the late twentieth century. Second, Marx and Lenin dealt with the formal colonial empires established and maintained by the great colonial powers of the 19th century. Dependency theorists are instead concerned with "neocolonialism" or the more informal systems of dominance maintained by the economic mechanisms of international capital rather than by direct political control.

One of the first post-war scholars to adapt these ideas to the post-war political system was Albert Hirschman (1945) in his analysis of foreign trade as an extension of nation-state power. Hirschman utilized a historical approach to support his thesis through a study of foreign economic policy in Nazi Germany. Hirschman argues that commerce can be an alternative to war as a policy for dominating other nations. Furthermore, Hirschman (1945, p. 15) argues that, "even if war could be eliminated, foreign trade would lead to relationships of dependence and influence between nations." Hence, trade becomes an instrument of domination rather than an item of mutual benefit as characterized by the liberal paradigm. Hirschman (1945, pp. 36-37) illustrates this dependent nature of trade through the following analysis of Nazi trade policy:

> Germany's attempt to concentrate on exports of finished products, on the one hand, and on exports to agricultural countries, on the other, had obviously the result of giving her exports a quasi-monopolistic position so far as the productive system of her trading partners was concerned. In addition, to maintain this position, it was one of the great principles of German foreign economic policy to prevent the industrialization of her agricultural trading partners. . . . By offering a stable market for the agricultural surplus production of these countries, she tied landowners and peasants, the most powerful social groups in these countries, to her own interests.

Two points are worth noting from this quotation. First, Hirschman describes what dependency theorists have since come to label as "unequal exchange," a trade relationship where dependent countries supply raw materials to the developed world and purchase finished manufactured products in return. Second, Hirschman argues that interests of the most powerful groups in the periphery became coincidental with interests of international capital. This too later becomes a central tenet of dependency theory. Finally, it should be noted that attempts by Germany to maximize its own national interest had an inadvertent detrimental effect on the periphery nations, much as dependency theorists would later argue. Hirschman did not infer that the results of his analysis of German trade policy were generalizable to other core-periphery relationships. That step was left to be taken by Raul Prebisch (1950, 1964) and Gunnar Myrdal (1957).

The dependency school of Prebisch and Myrdal developed out of Marxist thought as a reaction to the economic policies of the UN Economic Commission for Latin America (Love, 1990, pp. 1-2). By the early 1960's, it had become apparent to many, perhaps most notably one-time ECLA director Raul Prebisch, that the import substitution strategies advocated by the ECLA had not produced the desired economic growth (Prebisch, 1961, p. 24). As a result, by the late 1960's, the United Nations Conference on Trade and Development (UNCTAD) was urging LDCs to liberalize their trade policies and accept greater foreign investment and penetration (Girvan, 1973, p. 8). Subsequently, the liberalization of trade policies, similar to the policy of import substitution, was perceived among many Latin Americans as ineffective at stimulating growth. Furthermore, the liberalization of trade policies had the added adverse effect of rendering Latin American states more vulnerable to the fluctuations in the external international capitalist system (Prebisch, 1961, p. 5).

According to Prebisch (1950, 1964), the basic problem in core-periphery relations is the long-term decline in terms of trade. In other words, periphery nations were exporting primarily raw materials and importing primarily finished manufactured products from core nations. Prebisch contended that the price of manufactured goods tend to rise faster than those of raw materials, hence the decline in terms of trade. Furthermore, Prebisch (1950, 1964) argued that the strength of organized labor in the core tended to make the price of raw materials exported by the core to the periphery rise at a faster rate than raw material exports from the periphery, exacerbating the terms of trade problem. Prebisch's declining terms of trade argument was supported by a study from the International Bank for Reconstruction and Development (1974) which concluded that terms of trade in LDCs had consistently declined in the 1950-1971 period.

In order to counteract the terms of trade problem, Prebisch asserted that LDCs were forced to constantly increase their volume of exports as compared to their import volume in order to achieve a positive balance of payments. Unfortunately, periphery states were unable to increase their exports in relation to their imports, due to the inelasticity of demand for the raw materials which they produced (Prebisch, 1964). Consequently, Prebisch argued that the liberal free-market prescription would be unable to remedy the terms of trade problems for LDCs. In order to remedy this problem, Prebisch (1964) essentially prescribed that core states must subsidize periphery manufactured exports through nonreciprocal tariff reduction. Myrdal also argued that LDCs must retain high tariffs in order to substitute domestic goods for imports and bolster domestic manufacturing.

Regardless of which of the above strategies that international organizations prescribed at any particular time for Latin American growth, it is noteworthy that the prescriptions were structural in nature; therefore, it should not be surprising that a polemical structural perspective would arise to challenge the prescriptions of the Western-dominated international organizations. The general idea of the dependency perspective, that the expansion of the capitalist economies of the industrialized West impedes the growth of lesser developed states as a consequence, was also echoed by Gunnar Myrdal (1957). Myrdal argued that the international capitalist system left unregulated tended to increase the movement of finance capital and skilled labor from developed to lesser developed states. The higher the level of development by the core state, the greater the "spread" effect of the finance capital and skilled labor to the LDCs. Myrdal argues that this process produces uneven development between core and peripheral areas, which left unchecked, will increase inequalities both between the core and periphery and within both the core and periphery. In other words, Myrdal expects the core countries to grow at a faster rate than LDCs, thereby creating an ever larger income gap between core and periphery states. Simultaneously, within both core and periphery states, Myrdal expected the domestic income gap to continually increase.

Also similar to Prebisch, Myrdal (1970, p. 297) later argues that international trade produces inequality:

> International trade...will generally tend to breed inequality, and will do so the more strongly when substantial inequalities are already established ...Unregulated market forces will not work toward reaching any equilibrium which could imply a trend toward an equalization of incomes. By circular causation with cumulative effects, a country superior in productivity and income will tend to become more superior, while a country on an inferior level will tend to be held down at that level or even to deteriorate further-as long as matters are left to the free unfolding of the market forces.

Both Myrdal and Prebisch place emphasis on the vested interests of the core and structures placed in the periphery by the core during the colonial period as major obstacles to subsequent development in LDCs. Myrdal and Prebisch also both supported import substitution in their earlier writings, only to abandon that policy prescription in later writings (Myrdal, 1970; Prebisch, 1964). Myrdal and Prebisch also both inferred that cooperation was possible between core and periphery states in the area of development planning, and compromise could be reached, possibly boosting development in the periphery. Dependency theorists disputed this assumption following the publication of Frank's (1967) seminal work, *Capitalism and Underdevelopment in Latin America*. It was also following this publication that the discipline of political science became flooded with dependency literature.

Radical Dependency Literature

Richard Bath and Dilmus James (1976, p. 10) label a group of scholars who tend to hold to the positions of Andre Gunder Frank with little important deviation as "radical dependency theorists." The radical dependency perspective of Andre Gunder Frank and that of other radical dependency theorists, such as James Cockroft (1972), and Dale Johnson (1972), is a direct rebuttal of modernization theorists, such as David McClelland (1967) and Daniel Lerner

(1958) who viewed underdevelopment as resulting from internal causes. Reflecting the Leninists' imperialism perspective, the radical dependency advocates propose that LDCs cannot follow the western path to development because of their different histories. More specifically, the history of colonialism prevents LDCs from following the same paths as developed western states since this colonial experience drastically altered the infrastructures of LDCs (Frank, 1967, p. 96). The outcome of this historical process is an asymmetrical structure of relations between the center and periphery states, producing a widening gap in levels of development. Due to the differential returns from trade, the international capitalist system has produced a system of exchange between the center and periphery which is biased in favor of the core at the expense of the periphery, exacerbating international inequalities. Hence, underdevelopment is caused by exploitation of LDCs (the periphery) by industrialized nations (the core). The only way for dependent states to break out of this exploitive, dependent relationship is through socialist revolution. Perhaps the most important work from the radical dependency perspective is that of Frank (1967). This perspective will be reviewed extensively below.

Frank's work (1967) was particularly important to the development of dependency literature since it led to a great volume of similar writings by like-minded scholars and because it gave rise to lively debate between dependency advocates and other scholars who view the work of the dependency school less favorably (Mayer 1989, p. 93; Almond, 1987). Frank's work is typical of what Bath and James (1976, p. 10) refer to as the "radical dependency approach." In this work Frank enunciates positions that are central to those of virtually all radical dependency advocates, thereby providing a springboard on which the entire school of dependency was catapulted. Frank (1967, pp. 197-211) proposed that capitalism simultaneously produces underdevelopment in some areas and produces development in others. This approach has been adopted by dependency advocates in general (Chilcote and Edelstein, 1974, pp. 27-28), with a consensus that underdevelopment is produced in LDCs through contact with the West.

Frank (1967, pp. 197-211) also viewed the structure of the international capitalist system as a system of metropolis-satellite relationships which linked the United States (metropolis) with dependent states (satellites) and linked the elites of dependent states with their own interior in a dependent relationship, thus linking all areas of the world in a chain of dependency, class struggle, and unequal exchange. Additionally, the only method available for LDCs to break out of the dependent relationships was through socialist revolution (Frank, 1967, pp. 200-211). Frank is not alone in this prescription, but instead is joined by other radical writers (for example, see Cockroft, 1972; Johnson, 1972; Petras, 1973; Chilcote and Edelstein, 1974), as well as some more moderate writers, such as Theotonio Dos Santos (1970), in viewing socialist revolution as a sound policy choice for LDCs who desire to shed dependency and underdevelopment. In addition, Frank (1967) draws a distinction between underdeveloped and undeveloped. Frank (1967) contends that the industrialized west was never underdeveloped, a state which is only caused by contact between undeveloped states and developed states, since there were no developed states to exploit the underdeveloped west during their periods of development. Frank's position has also been widely adopted by other dependency scholars (Chilcote and Edelstein, 1974, pp. 27-28). In this view, the political, social, and economic structures and situations of LDCs are argued to be qualitatively different from those of western industrialized states during their periods of development since modern LDCs are externally shaped by developed states and their developmental destinies are completely out of their own control (Chilcote and Edelstein, 1974; Frank, 1972, p. 318). Indeed, it is this external shaping of social, political, and economic structures which defines dependency as evidenced by the following, widely quoted dependency definition offered by Dos Santos (1970).

> By dependence we mean a situation in which the economy of certain countries is conditioned by the development and expansion of another economy to which the former is subjected. The relation of interdependence between two or more economies, and between these and world trade, assumes the form of dependence when some countries (the dominant ones) can expand and can be self-sustaining, while other countries (the dependent ones) can do this only as a reflection of that expansion, which can have either a positive or a negative effect on their immediate development.

According to Frank (1967), since the economic well-being of LDCs is shaped by the world capitalist system and their relationships with external industrialized states, the situation in the Third World is best described as the "development of underdevelopment," a process divided into four stages, each defined by the principal form of monopoly exercised by the metropolis: commercial monopoly or mercantilism prior to 1800, industrial monopoly 1800-1900, monopoly of capital goods 1900-1950, and technological monopoly 1950 to present. Bath and James (1976), in a review of dependency literature, conclude that there is general agreement among dependency scholars that technological dependence is a major aspect of dependency.

Frank (1967) also argues that the bourgeoisie in dependent states is divided into two segments: one associated with the international sector, and another associated with the domestic sector. Frank posits that the international sector bourgeoisie are the most powerful and control the most dynamic industries because of access to international capital. The domestic sector bourgeoisie within LDCs are subordinate to the international sector bourgeoisie within LDCs whose interests coincide with those of the international capitalists in the metropolis. The lower classes in LDCs are living in poverty and have no political power. As a result, power is concentrated in the hands of a few internationally oriented elites, therefore lending itself to authoritarian rule. The masses and domestic bourgeoisie are too weak to establish democratic institutions. Furthermore, the interests of the international bourgeoisie are opposed to those of society as a whole; therefore, authoritarian rule is necessarily instituted by the international bourgeoisie in order to control society (Frank, 1967, pp. 43-53). This central argument that the bourgeoisie or elites in LDCs have similar interests to, and are controlled by, elites in the industrialized core has become another major area of consensus among dependency scholars (Bath and James, 1976, 11; Chilcote and Edelstein, 1974, pp. 30-32, 53).

Frank's perspective is a direct rebuttal of the modernization position that underdevelopment is the result of internal causes. Reflecting the Leninists' imperialism perspective, the radical dependency advocates propose that LDCs cannot follow the western path to development because of their different histories. More specifically, the history of colonialism prevents LDCs from following the same paths as developed western states since this colonial experience drastically altered the infrastructures of LDCs (Frank, 1967, p. 96; Cardoso and Faletto, 1979, p. 23). Frank argues that these historical and economic processes which create development in the Western metropolis simultaneously create underdevelopment in the satellites. Dependency, according to Frank, is merely a stage in the development of the world capitalist system. However, rather than viewing this dependency as a stage on the path to industrialization, Frank views the satellites' underdevelopment as a stage in development of the world capitalist system which would continue to retard development in the Third World. In the words of Frank, "they are rich, because we are poor" (1967, p. 97).

In summation, Frank's four most important hypotheses, as presented by Alvin So (1990), are presented below:

> Hypothesis #1. In contrast to the development of the world metropolis, which is no one's satellite, the development of national and other subordinate metropolises is limited by other satellite statuses. For instance, although Sao Paulo has begun to build up an industrial establishment, Frank does not believe Brazil can break out of the cycle of satellite development, which is characterized by non-autonomous and unsatisfactory industrial development.

> Hypothesis #2. The satellites experience their greatest economic development when their ties to the metropolis are weakest.

> Hypothesis #3. When the metropolis recovers from its crisis, and re-establishes the trade and investment ties that then fully reincorporate the satellites into the system, the previous industrialization of these regions is choked off.

> Hypothesis #4. The regions that are the most underdeveloped
> today are those that had the closest ties to the metropolises in
> the past. Archaic institutions in the satellites are historical
> products of the penetration of metropolis capitalism. (So,
> 1990, pp. 97-98)

In Frank's analysis, there is no room for development within the dependent satellites which are merely economic colonies of the metropolis. In later works, Frank (1972, p. 318) takes his position that capitalist expansion produces underdevelopment even farther, arguing that the earlier and more persistent the contacts between LDCs and capitalistic institutions, the more underdeveloped lesser developed states are likely to be. Essentially then, Frank's position is the direct opposite of that of liberal modernization theorists.

Frank's work led to a flood of similar works from other scholars who tend to accept Frank's perspective. Ronald Chilcote and Joel Edelstein (1974), James Cockroft (1972, 1974), Johan Galtung (1971), Dale Johnson (1972), and James Petras (1973) are representatives who are in concurrence with Frank, taking the position that the interests of the core and the periphery are "definitely opposed" rather than complementary. Importantly, virtually all kinds of contact with the industrialized West, including foreign aid and foreign investment, according to them, are viewed as detrimental to LDCs (Chilcote and Edelstein, 1974, p. 27; Bath and James, 1976, p. 11).

Significant among these radical dependency scholars is the approach of Johan Galtung (1971). Like Frank, Galtung based his formulation on a center-periphery model of the international system. Galtung divides the global system into four hierarchical classes with the elites within the most developed states at the top, elites in LDCs underneath them, masses in developed states a notch lower, and the masses within the least developed states at the bottom. Galtung views dependency as a facet of imperialism and offers the following definition of imperialism (1971, p. 83):

> Imperialism is a relation between a Center and a Periphery nation so
> that (1) there is harmony of interest between the center in the Center
> nations and the center in the Periphery nation, (2) there is more
> disharmony of interest within the Periphery nation than within the
> Center nation, (3) there is disharmony of interest between the
> periphery in the Center nation and the periphery in the Periphery
> nation.

Galtung's first element of imperialism, harmony of interests between core elites and periphery elites, is labeled by Paul Baran (1957) as clientelism. This clientelism tends to be viewed by dependency theorists as a major impediment to development in LDCs since the interests of elites in both the core and periphery are viewed as contradictory to the needs of the lower class in the periphery.

Similar to Frank, in Galtung's writings, the processes at work which create development in the center and underdevelopment for the periphery are circular and cumulative. Additionally, Galtung concurs with Frank that only through the displacement of the center by the periphery can these processes be overcome. This assessment is essentially just another way of stating that dependency can be severed only through socialist revolution.

Despite Galtung's "structural approach," dependency (or imperialism in his formulation) still suffers from a high degree of abstraction that renders it unreceptive to scientific methodology. Secondly, Galtung's formulation, like Frank's, remains quite deterministic in character, and fails to explain the apparent development during the 1960's in many LDCs, particularly the newly industrializing countries (NICs) of Asia (Bath and James, 1976, p. 11).

New Dependency

Although dependency advocates generally tend to support the contentions of Frank, something of a paradigm shift has taken place within dependency literature since 1970 led by the work of Cardoso (1973), Cardoso and Faletto (1979), and Peter Evans (1976, 1979). Scholars who have produced this paradigm shift are labeled by Alvin So (1990) as "New Dependency" scholars. The "New Dependency" perspective surfaced primarily due to the inability of radical dependency theorists to explain increases in growth and economic development in LDCs. Such an argument is central to that of Cardoso and Faletto (1979, pp. 17, 28, 38), who coined the term "associated-dependent development" to refer to such phenomena.

Associated-dependent development, according to Cardoso (1973), refers to a process of externally induced economic growth within LDCs which is achieved by curtailing or reducing domestic consumption and welfare. The policies which produce associated-dependent development are produced from liberal capitalist economic theories which stress capital formation. According to Cardoso (1973), policymakers in LDCs attract foreign investment by providing low wages and other incentives to investors. The foreign investment then may provide robust, but uneven, growth.

Cardoso (1973, p. 149) argues that "to some extent, the interests of the foreign corporations become compatible with the internal prosperity of the dependent country. In this sense, they help promote development." Although Cardoso and Faletto (1979) argue that a form of development for LDCs is possible in spite of dependency, such "associated dependent development" tends to lead to bureaucratic authoritarianism because of a political alliance between elite interests in the core and elite interests in the periphery. According to Cardoso (in Bonilla and Girling, 1973, pp. 7-16), the type of development in dependent economies "creates a restricted, limited and upper class oriented type of market and society." Furthermore, Cardoso (in Bonilla and Girling, 1973, p. 13) describes dependent development as "contradictory, exploitive, and generates inequalities." Cardoso (1973, p. 176) also argues that associated dependent development may lead to an increase in the accumulation of wealth, but leads to "mass manipulation" and will not bring about development "favoring the majority and increasing the quality of life." Cardoso does not, however, explain what he means by "quality of life."

Peter Evans (1976) supports the associated-dependent development thesis through the application of a case study approach to the Brazilian economy of the 1960's. Evans reveals a shift in the Brazilian economy during this period away from primary products and toward manufactured products which were financed largely by foreign capital. Evans documented robust growth for Brazilian manufacturing during the period, but also documented increased inequality. The inference, of course, is that Brazilian growth was being achieved through increased exploitation of the working class.

Cardoso and Faletto (1979) argue against a "theory of dependency" and state that different "situations of dependency" exist. The basic argument is that the exact nature of dependency depends on the nature of alliances between governmental elites, foreign capitalists, and other prominent economic and political groups internal to the societies. A similar conclusion is reached by Susan Bodenheimer (1970, p. 357), who concludes that dependent indus-trialization is integrated into and complementary to the needs of foreign economies and that clientele social classes in the periphery have a vested interest in the goals of the capitalists in the core.

Cardoso and Faletto (1979, p. xviii) state that their purpose is to show "how internal and external processes of political domination relate to one another" and how "external factors are interwoven with internal ones . . . . to determine the links between social groups." In other words, the economic dependency of LDCs stems not only from the domination by external forces, but also from the much more complex interaction of economic forces, political structures, social movements, and historically conditioned alliances.

Cardoso and Faletto take a historical approach to support their arguments presenting examples of societies whose economies developed differently due to varying political alliances. Cardoso and Faletto allow greater latitude to elites in LDCs in making development decisions than do their radical dependency counterparts. Furthermore, Cardoso and Faletto (1979, p. 196) point out that LDCs have often been able to exert influence over core nations in procuring favorable treaties and credit lines. Supporting the work of Cadoso and Faletto, Evans (1979) argues that decision-makers in LDCs have the freedom to make political choices about economic development within the constraints of dependent relationships. Similarly, Martin Staniland (1985) cites the decisions of governmental elites in Brazil to develop industry to alleviate economic sluggishness. Essentially, the argument is that increases in levels of development and industrialization can occur, although that development is "dependent" on support from external forces and less efficient than indigenously led development. In these analyses, the state and other prominent economic elites, which benefit from development in the economic sectors they control, provide the means through which core states are able to develop at the expense of LDCs while allowing some form of development in LDCs.

Cardoso (1973), Cardoso and Faletto (1979), and Guillermo O'Donnell (1973, 1979) argue that this "associated dependent development" results in uneven development and economic inequality within the LDCs; consequently, authoritarian regimes are instilled in order to control the disturbances. Hence, these new dependency scholars infer that authoritarianism is necessary in LDCs in order to achieve the type of development which is produced in dependent economies. Similarly, Ronaldo Munck (1985) argues that external dependency forces LDCs to accept a situation where their own development and the capital accumulation of core states are inextricably linked. The political ramifications of this situation are that state regimes were forced to develop in order to reconcile these "opposing" goals. Consequently, populist regimes were replaced with bureaucratic-authoritarian regimes.

Although the work of new dependency scholars is much less deterministic than those of the radical dependency approach, and they do provide examples of differing forms of dependency produced by diverse configurations of state and class alliances, the thread which binds them to the radical approach is the contention that external factors remain major determinants of economic "under-development." Cardoso and Faletto (1979) argue that when there are economic or political crises in the core, LDCs tend to adopt policies targeting internal development. As an example, they cite the actions of Latin American states during World War II when they essentially followed an import substitution strategy, imposing tariffs to boost the domestic sector and fund the establishment of state-owned steel and oil industries and electrical power plants (Cardoso and Faletto, 1979, p. 129). Additionally, although Cardoso (1973) criticizes the deterministic nature of radical dependency scholarship, Cardoso (1973) and Cardoso and Faletto (1979) use deterministic language themselves in their unbending arguments that dependency produces income inequality, authoritarianism, and depressed quality of life.

Cardoso and Faletto also place great stock in the role of multinational corporations as agents of dependency. Essentially, they argue that the rise of multinational corporations has placed greater economic restrictions on development in LDCs. In the words of Cardoso and Faletto,

> The linkages between the dependent economies and the internationalization of the market have solidified through the creation of industrial platforms for the export of products where MNCs seek a comparative advantage, the transformation of colonial enclaves into those of imperialist corporations, concentration of isolated production processes, and the control of local markets by MNC production. (1979, p. 187)

Building on the work of Cardoso and Faletto, Munck (1985) argues that development in LDCs is directed by, and dependent on, foreign capital and interests. Evans (1979) also views multinational corporations (MNCs) as having great importance in constraining the dependent states. Evans credits MNCs with transferring technical knowledge, finances, and liberal values to the state in Brazil; however, Evans allows the state a more independent role in economic development. In Evans' work, a "triple alliance" emerges consisting of the state, MNCs, and local capitalists, all working together for the purpose of national development and profits. Similarly, Richard Sklar (1987) argues that a "managerial bourgeoisie" develops in LDCs consisting of MNCs, and domestic and international-oriented capitalists within LDCs. Like Evans, Sklar argues that the state and capitalists in LDCs are "socialized" by foreign capitalists to adopt liberal values. Although these "new dependency" scholars recognize that economic growth and industrialization are possible in dependent economies, they argue that the dependent growth leads to the strengthening of the state productive sector and creates increasingly repressive states.

Similar to radical dependency theorists, new dependency theorists tend to be supportive of the position that the chains of dependency can only be broken through a transition to socialism. Cardoso and Faletto (1979, p. 213), for example, argue that the only alternative to dependent development is the adoption of socialism, albeit difficult.

In summation, dependency theory has evolved to encompass the possibility that some form of development may occur in dependent relationships; however, the development is inequitable and benefits only the elites. Furthermore, dependency theorists argue that increases in industrialization and growth in LDCs do not lead to any basic changes in the structures of dominance and dependence between core and periphery states. This position is well articulated by Dos Santos (1976, p. 86):

> The new phase of big capital, relying on multinational corporations, leads to a new international division of labor which presupposes an increase in the industrialization of raw materials and of products of a low degree of technological development, and the export of these products to the dominant centers, particularly to the United States which, in its turn would specialize in the production of goods and services for export which have a high technological content, and the export of capital, thus raising the parasitism typical of the imperialist powers to its highest level.

In other words, Dos Santos argues that associated-dependent development will exacerbate unequal exchange and technological dependency with all of the negative long term effects still prevalent. Dos Santos (1976) refers to this continuance of structures of dominance and dependency as "neo-colonialism," a term which describes the set of mechanisms which reinforce the exploitive system supposedly established during the colonial period. According to Dos Santos, the three most important of these mechanisms are clientelism (when needs and goals of elites in LDCs coincide with those of international capital), aid, and multinational corporations.

One final comment is necessary on the prospect that development is possible in LDCs in dependent relationships. Definitions of development among dependency scholars do not necessarily refer to growth and industrialization. Frank (1972, p. 28) argues that GNP growth is not what he means by development at all; rather, development is equated with equity, which he argues dependency fails to produce. However, both radical dependency theorists and new dependency theorists glaringly omit the possibility that physical quality of life may be unaffected by greater inequality.

General Consensus

Several principles emerge from dependency literature as enjoying broad consensus among dependency scholars. Essentially, consensus has emerged on the following propositions: development is outside of the control of LDCs, and underdevelopment is externally caused; unequal exchange is a major mechanism for perpetuating and exacerbating underdevelopment; internationally oriented elites are the only class benefiting from the dependent economy structure within LDCs; what development may occur in dependent states is contradictory in character and produces gross income inequalities; dependent economies tend to produce bureaucratic authoritarian governments; the only method for eradicating dependency is socialist revolution. These elements of this broad-based consensus will be discussed below.

Chilcote and Edelstein (1974) argue that consensus has emerged as to the consequences of dependency. The effects of dependency presented by Chilcote and Edelstein (1974) are:

1. The prosperity and growth of a dependent economy is primarily a function of international economic and political events over which no domestic economic or political actors can exert any substantial degree of control.

2. Dependency results in a long term net capital drain on the LDC. Through a variety of mechanisms, the economic surplus of the LDC is transferred to the developed countries, thus accounting for the inability of the LDCS to generate sustained economic growth.

2.(a) A principal mechanism through which economic surplus of the LDC is transferred to developed countries involves unequal exchange, the idea that raw commodities are exported from LDCs to the core, and finished manufactured goods are imported from the core to LDCs.

3. The responsiveness of the dependent economy to external
factors yields domestic benefits only to the few who mediate
the country's international economic relations, while the
absence of inner-directed development leaves the bulk of the
people in severe deprivation.

These principles could, perhaps, be summed up by the following
statements: underdevelopment in LDCs is produced through external causes;
unequal exchange is central to the production and perpetuation of
underdevelopment; and only internationally-oriented elites in LDCs benefit from
dependency.

Essentially, all dependency theorists, whether radicals (Frank, 1967;
Cockroft, 1972; Johnson, 1972; Petras, 1973) or "new dependency" scholars
(Cardoso and Faletto, 1979; Evans, 1979), argue that development is to a large
extent outside the control of LDCs. This is the essence of the very definition of
dependency as evidenced by the Dos Santos (1970) definition enunciated earlier.
Consequently, the state of underdevelopment must also be, for the most part,
externally caused. Several means are proposed by dependency theorists through
which core nations economically exploit and shape the periphery, and central to
this argument is the concept of unequal exchange. According to dependency
theorists, the core economies need to acquire raw materials cheaply and
simultaneously need markets for finished manufactured goods. LDCs are used
by the developed core to satisfy both needs with raw materials being shipped
from the periphery to the core and finished manufactured products exported
from the core to the periphery (Chilcote and Edelstein, 1974; Prebisch, 1961;
Bath and James, 1976; Love, 1990). This unequal exchange relationship is
central to dependency and the perpetuation of underdevelopment since
dependency theorists argue that prices of raw materials normally rise at a much
slower pace than the prices of manufactured goods (Prebisch, 1961).
Consequently, under such unequal trade relationships, LDCs can expect
negative trade balances to grow over the long term even if raw material
production increases steadily since raw material prices can be expected to
significantly lag behind the spiraling costs of finished manufactured products.
The task at hand then is to examine whether dependency does slow growth and
increase inequality over the long haul and whether elites in LDCs are the only
segment of the population who reap benefits.

There is also a consensus among new dependency scholars (Cardoso and
Faletto, 1979; Evans, 1979; O'Donnell, 1979) that dependency produces
inequality since the only segment of society which benefits in a dependent
economy are the internationally-oriented elites whose interests coincide with the
core interests. Furthermore, the structural dislocations of a dependent economy,
namely inequality, produce political unrest which requires bureaucratic-
authoritarian structures to quiet it. Finally, both radical dependency scholars

(Frank, 1967; Cockroft, 1972) and new dependency scholars (Cardoso and Faletto, 1979) argue that there is no escape from dependency except through a transition to socialism.

There appears to be no consensus among dependency theorists as to how dependency could be measured. This lack of consensus is one of the major criticisms of the dependency perspective which will be discussed below.

Disagreements

The dependency perspective is not without its detractors, nor are we the first to illuminate its possible shortcomings. In this section, the ideas and arguments of some of the major critics of the dependency perspective are presented and summarized. Criticisms leveled against the dependency framework include allegations that it is nothing more than political propaganda, is tautological, and poorly conceptualized. Dependency is charged with being poorly defined, based on insufficient evidence, and inconclusive. Dependency theorists have also been charged with ignoring dependency relationships between socialist "metropoles" and "satellites." Furthermore, although dependency is essentially grounded in the Marxist paradigm, noted scholars have criticized dependency for its inconsistency with Marx. It must be noted, however, that the major critics of the dependency paradigm tend to be liberal rather than Marxist scholars. Consequently, the following is a brief review of the more important disagreements with the dependency framework.

Michael Brown (1974) argues that dependency theorists are unable to explain how, in the first place, some states became developed and others did not. Brown illuminates the fact that the vast majority of the underdeveloped world was underdeveloped in relation to the core prior to contact between core and periphery and the colonial period which followed.

Gabriel Almond (1987) argues that the dependency perspective should not be considered theory at all, but rather is merely an exercise in pamphleteering or propaganda. David Ray (1973) argues that the dependency perspective suffers from several logical flaws; some dependency advocates such as Frank (1967) conceptualize dependency as a dichotomous variable, dependency being an either all or none situation, a conceptualization which destroys the policy relevance of dependency analysis. Concurring with Ray, Sanjaya Lall (1975) argues that dependency theorists have been unable to demonstrate either logically or empirically that dependent economies are qualitatively different in type from non-dependent economies and that the characteristics of dependency have an adverse effect on economic development. Lall argues that the failure to show that dependent economies are of a qualitatively different kind leaves open the possibility that development is a sequential stage phenomenon consistent with modernization theory. Hence, dependency, according to Lall, cannot rule out the possibility that differences in development between the developed and underdeveloped world are merely a matter of degree, rather than of a qualitatively different type. Lall (1975, pp. 800-807) observes that there are numerous characteristics shared by both developed and underdeveloped states such as reliance on foreign investment, foreign technology, and foreign sources of media information. Lall, therefore, concludes that dependency is a matter of degree rather than type and that it ranges on a continuum from the most powerful, least dependent state to the least powerful, most dependent state. Furthermore, Lall argues that the problems of dependent growth, such as inequality, debt, and trade imbalances, are shared by both developed and underdeveloped states.

Ray (1973) also argues that dependency theorists work with a biased sample since they ignore dependent economies in the former Communist bloc. This biased sample leads dependency theorists to come to the invalid conclusion that dependency is caused by capitalism when "simple disparity in power" is able to explain equally both dependency in the capitalist world as well as in the former Communist bloc (Ray, 1973, p. 7). Concurring with Ray is Robert Packenham (1973) who argues that the dependency framework ignores the core-periphery relationships between the former Soviet Union and its "satellites." As Packenham (1973) demonstrated through his Cuban case study, socialist revolution appears to be a poor way to sever bonds of dependency. Finally, Ray argues that the dependency argument that direct foreign investment produces underdevelopment is too simplistic. Essentially, Ray argues that while investment in some types of industries (such as resource extraction) may distort development, investment in other industries such as manufacturing or the service sector may not have distorting effects on development.

In a similar vein, Phillip O'Brien (1975) argues that dependency theses are often overstated, over-generalized, vague, and full of unsubstantiated reasoning, such as the suggestion that multinational corporations can repatriate all of the profits from enterprises in LDCs. Alec Nove (1975) concurs with O'Brien, arguing that radical dependency theorists destroy their own case through broad overstatements and omission of solid evidence. Nove further chastises dependency theorists for ignoring the role of internal factors such as domestic politics, population demographics, and culture. Nove adds that the most serious flaw in dependency theory is the failure to distinguish between the concept of "underdevelopment" and foreign political and economic control or exploitation.

Taking a somewhat different approach, Gabriel Almond (1987) criticizes dependency theory for misuse of Marxism. Almond argues that dependency theorists tend to adhere to Marxist paradigms of historic materialism, yet the historical evidence that should accompany a historic materialist argument is often slim or nonexistent. For their part, Marx and Engels (1955, p. 14) argue that

> The bourgeoisie, by the rapid improvement of all instruments of production, by the immensely facilitated means of communication, draws all nations, even the most barbarian into civilization. . . . It

compels all nations . . . . to adopt the bourgeois mode of production;
it compels them to . . . . become bourgeois themselves.

This statement suggests that Marx and Engels expected contact between core states and the periphery to produce development in the periphery, contrary to the views of Frank (1967). Lenin (1960) argues that capitalist states will spread capitalism to the periphery in order to exploit the cheap labor. Lenin explained that capitalism, by nature, had to expand in order to siphon off surplus value; therefore, the core would develop markets in the periphery and acquire raw materials from the periphery. Essentially then, Lenin, Marx and Engels declare that capitalism contains the seeds of its own destruction and the core will destroy itself by spreading its capitalism to the periphery, which subsequently develops and surpasses the core. It is, perhaps, ironic then that empirical testing of the dependency perspective cannot simultaneously support both the dependency position that periphery-core contact produces periphery underdevelopment and the Marxist-Leninist position that periphery-core contact will develop the periphery at the expense of the core.

The dependency perspective is also criticized for often being very poorly operationalized (Lall, 1975; Nove, 1975; Obrien, 1975; Mayer, 1989). This poor operationalization is contended to produce tautological arguments. Lall (1975) contends that the arguments of Frank (1967) and other radical dependency theorists essentially follow the tautological circle. The basic argument becomes that dependent countries are those which lack the capacity for autonomous growth because they are dependent.

In addition to these criticisms leveled against dependency theory, we contribute further criticism. Essentially, we argue that the associated dependent development argument neglects the progress in LDCs over the last three decades in improving physical quality of life. Dependency theorists argue that dependency produces inequality. Implicit in this argument is the contention that the lower class suffers greater hardship due to dependency. While we dispute the contention that dependency produces inequality to begin with, we argue that such inequality that does exist is likely to be produced by an increasing rate of growth of the wealth of the upper income class in LDCs, vis-a-vis slower growth of the wealth of the lower class. In other words, when inequality increases, it does not necessarily mean that the lower class has experienced decreased physical quality of life; it simply means that the income gap between them and the wealthier class has increased. On the contrary, the physical quality of life of the lower class may even be improved as inequality increases if their standard of living has improved in an absolute sense, although simultaneously worsening in a relative sense to that of the wealthier class. Furthermore, we argue that contact with the core increases the quality of life in LDCs as indicated by literacy, life expectancy and infant mortality rates due to the introduction of more modern medical practices and humanitarian assistance.

Chapter 3

Measurement and Empirical Studies

Measuring Dependency

Although dependency or certain aspects of dependency have been subjected to empirical analysis in numerous instances, there is disagreement among scholars over the ability to measure the concept. Cardoso and Faletto (1979, pp. 22-23), argue that

> it is a mistaken approach, for instance, to test hypotheses about the effects, let us say, of associated-development on income distribution in situations of dependency based on the penetration of multinational corporations in the sector of mass consumption production, constructing the "independent variable," using aggregate data. . . . No statistical result extracted from such an amalgam can prove or disprove any statement on dependence because the basic assumption of such a formal methodology dissolves the differences in situations of dependency and these are key notions for the historic-structural approach.

Clearly, Cardoso and Faletto view dependence as a situation which is unsuitable to empirical analysis. This conception of dependency appears to be an "all or none" type situation and not a matter of variable degree. Hence, such a conception disallows any conception of degrees of dependency or the possibility that states may somehow lessen dependency without eliminating it completely. Consequently, Cardoso and Faletto strongly oppose anything other than a historical structural analysis of dependency.

It must be noted, however, that Cardoso and Faletto (1979, p. 21) also discuss "situations of extreme dependency." If "dependency" can be labeled as extreme, then it can also be labeled as less extreme or mild. Hence, although Cardoso and Faletto argue that dependency is not a term that should be conceptualized as a continuum and empirically analyzed as such, their own discussion essentially treats dependency as a continuum that at the very least ranges from extreme dependency to less extreme. As a consequence, their own conceptualization of dependency is suitable for empirical analysis through the use of modern quantitative methods.

Other notable scholars, such as Dos Santos (1970) and Raymond Duvall (1978) also avoid the empirical testing of dependency. Dos Santos (1970, p. 31) contends that dependence itself does not explain or account for development. On the contrary, Dos Santos argues that "in the context of dependence, development is to be explained by other phenomena." Duvall (1978, pp. 58-59) favors the historical-structural approach, arguing that:

> the almost universal representation of dependencia theory . . . . as a theory about the relationship between dependence and development (or underdevelopment) is an unfortunate and misleading representation . . . . . The common implication is that development is affected by dependence, in which case the latter is transformed into a (central) concept in theory, and hence, is nothing more than a variable property of countries or of relationships among countries. Such a representation reflects a fundamental misunderstanding of the meaning of dependence for dependencia theory and distorts tremendously the nature of that theory.

Hence, Duvall, like Cardoso and Faletto, does not view dependency as a variable property which can be measured. Duvall (1978, p. 60) views dependency as a qualitatively distinct form of relationship which can only be analyzed through "descriptive analysis of historical processes of social transformation." Duvall contends that the dependency perspective "places primary emphasis on concrete analysis, and detailed, historical, descriptive, contextually-bound knowledge claims." Duvall (1978, p. 68) purports that indicators which tap the extent and concentration of physical transactions of countries do not tap the "forms and extent of metropole capitalist penetration," and instead asserts that the best such indicators can do is tap the "media or mechanisms of contingency and/or the potential for subordination or support." In short, Duvall (1978, p. 55), quoting Cardoso and Faletto, argues that the only way to understand dependence is through "dialectical analysis of concrete situations of dependence."

In a similar vein, James Caporaso (1980) draws a distinction between "dependence," defined as external reliance on other actors, and "dependency," defined as the process of incorporation of LDCs into the global capitalist system and the resulting "structural distortions." Caporaso argues that the "dependence" orientation explores the asymmetries among nation-states. Caporaso (1980, p. 2) states that "dependence is a term which can be meaningfully discussed at the dyadic level . . . . thus, dependence theory is easily linked to statistical modes of analysis." However, Caporaso contradicts himself in explaining that statistical analysis of dependency is to be avoided. Caporaso argues that the "dependency" orientation focuses on class relations both within LDCs and in an international sense and the role of the state in managing national and international class relations. This structural perspective, argues Caporaso, rejects the concept of the state as a unified actor, making it difficult to conceive of dependency in dyadic patterns for statistical analysis. Although Caporaso states that there is "no reason, in principle, that dependency cannot be statistically tested," the fact that it is a world-wide and historical phenomenon prevents it from being reduced to a dyad and necessitates its being measured across time. In the words of Caporaso, underdeveloped countries are conceptualized as:

Qualitatively different expressions of capitalism at the global level-not as variations (hence magnitudes along a unidimensional continuum). Hence, hypotheses about relationships between the degree of dependency and dependent variables cannot be evaluated inside this framework, while propositions about historical qualitiative transformations (e.g., from slave plantation to mercantile dependency) can be assessed . . . . In short, the historical constraint removes temporal degrees of freedom while the global penetration assumption removes cross-sectional variability. Both constraints reduce the independent variation of concepts in the theory and prevent the cumulation of large distributions which can then be paired and scrutinized in some form of covariance analysis. (1980, p. 3)

We take issue with several of the above arguments. First, are we to accept that the only method for investigating dependency is "dialectical analysis of concrete situations of dependence" as Duvall (1978, p. 55) has suggested? If so, then what other phenomena are limited solely to this type of analysis? War? Political violence? Voting behavior? By the same logic, these other phenomena could also be only viewed through dialectical analysis. If dialectical analysis is the only acceptable framework for analysis, then the whole of mainstream political science must be discarded. In other words, everyone is out of step except dependency theorists who analyze all phenomena through a historical-structural framework.

Second, Caporaso admits that dependency is "relational," and therefore if those relations exist, they must be measurable. Third, the fact that dependency is a world-wide phenomenon does not necessarily reduce the degrees of freedom; instead, it merely suggests that dependency be measured on a global, rather than regional basis. Fourth, we argue that the measurement of dependency over time is possible and that this measurement over time will capture the concept of dependency as a process and the "context" of dependency which the theorists stress. Furthermore, though Caporaso may (or may not) be correct in his assertion that dependency is a qualitatively different form of capitalism, this does not preclude comparison. Consider, for example, Adam Przeworski and Henry Teune's (1970) famous fruit analogy where they essentially argue that one can compare qualitatively different entities such as oranges and apples, which are both fruit; both have skin, both have juice, both have seeds, etc. Finally, since Caporaso states that the "umbrella concept" underlying both "dependence" and "dependency" is relational inequality, this concept can then be tapped through indicators which reflect relational inequality such as measures of unequal exchanges.

Although we agree with Caporaso's (1980) assessment that the term dependency is complex but often imprecise, there is a general agreement that the term "dependency" refers to "asymmetric properties of the structure of relationships among social entities" (Duvall, 1978, p. 55). If this is indeed what dependency is, then these asymmetric properties and their effects are observable and measurable. Furthermore, Cardoso (1973, p. 149) himself argues that "to some extent the interests of the foreign corporations become compatible with the internal prosperity of the dependent country. In this sense, they help promote development." This statement by Cardoso clearly implies causation and contradicts the view that dependency is not a matter of degree. Finally, if dependency cannot be measured, then why have dependency advocates, such as Peter Evans and Michael Timberlake (1979), subjected aspects of dependency to empirical analysis in order to support the perspective? In fact, Duvall himself, in a study with several noted scholars (Duvall et al., 1983), empirically analyzes a form of a dependency relationship and constructs variables for measuring what they term the "coercive authoritarianism of the peripheral state." Duvall and his associates utilize the size of the military, percentage of cabinet posts and above held by military personnel, the number of political prisoners, and a media-based indicator of the frequency and severity of coercive negative sanctions targeted at "social collectivities." The point which is illustrated by this laundry list of variables is not that they are invalid, but that they are not qualitatively different than the indicators utilized by non-dependency scholars in empirical analyses of dependency; therefore, they are no more able to tap any underlying abstract historical-structural condition than those utilized by non-dependency scholars. This does not mean that such indicators are useless. At the very least, such indicators offer evidence that peripheral countries do vary widely in the extent and concentration of their external ties to the core, and as such, empirical analysis may be employed to explain these variances.

A further incongruity in dependency literature is the assessment by Duvall (1978) that dependency is so holistic in character that elements of dependency cannot be isolated. If this position is correct, then Duvall and his associates (Duvall et al., 1983) cannot isolate elements of dependency such as "coercive authoritarianism of the peripheral state" and analyze them separately. Duvall (1978, p. 58) himself labels the usage of terms such as "technological dependency" or "cultural dependency" as "secondary usage" which creates a "real ambiguity," but then argues that such secondary usages do not infer that dependency can be measured. If such is the case, then it is difficult to see where Duvall et al. (1983) derived the notion that they could measure "coercive authoritarianism of the peripheral state," which appears to be a "secondary usage" of "dependency." As this discussion above illustrates, arguments that dependency cannot be measured suffer from a number of weaknesses. Certainly, if the concept of dependency cannot be captured in full, aspects of dependency such as penetration by multinational corporations, unequal exchange, and debt, are measureable and may be able to explain a significant portion of the variance in growth, inequality, and physical quality of life. Although these indicators may only tap "secondary usages," they can be applied to a multitude of countries over an extended time frame. This type of longitudinal, cross-national, empirical analysis in itself seems much more "holistic" than the historical case study approach which dependency theorists seem to be advocating.

Empirical analysis of the relationship between dependency indicators and development is valuable to the body of knowledge in political science, as a whole, even if the arguments of Duvall and Caporaso are correct and dependency cannot be captured through empirical analysis. As Dolan and Tomlin (1980, p. 41) explain, empirical analysis of the relationship between dependency and development focuses attention on the "effects of various forms of economic linkages on rates and types of economic development." This empirical analysis should produce new empirical knowledge concerning various forms of economic linkages. The results which are achieved from the analysis are valuable to the body of knowledge even if they are not accepted by radical dependency theorists as produced from a valid test of dependency.

As will be shown below, scholars in general have disregarded the arguments of dependency theorists that dependency cannot be measured. On the contrary, over the past quarter century, the dependency perspective has received a great deal of attention from empirical researchers who have attempted to test all or some facets of dependency theory. The highlights of this vast body of literature will be reviewed below.

Empirical Studies

Below is a review of the literature surrounding the empirical investigation of dependency theory. The review both illuminates the state of the discipline regarding empirical analysis of dependency theory and exposes the incomplete nature of the empirical research to date. First, the literature surrounding dependency and growth are reviewed, followed by the literature based on the relationship between dependency and inequality and other empirical studies of dependency. The general results, conclusions, and deficiencies of the literature are presented and discussed with the conclusion that more empirical research is merited.

As will be shown below, most studies on dependency have investigated either the relationship between dependency and growth or the relationship between dependency and inequality. No studies have investigated the relationship between dependency and the Physical Quality of Life Index (PQLI) or PQLI growth. Most empirical studies do not investigate dependency per se, but merely some aspect of dependency, such as penetration by multinational corporations. First, we will review the studies which focus on economic growth.

Dependency and Economic Growth

In general, as far as dependency is concerned, scholars have been concerned with the impact of dependency on economic growth. Numerous studies have investigated this relationship in one form or another (Alschuler, 1976; Bornschier et al., 1978; Bornschier and Ballmer-Cao, 1979; Bornschier, 1980; Chase-Dunn, 1975; Dolan and Tomlin, 1980; Gobalet and Diamond, 1979; Jackman, 1982; Kaufman et al., 1975; McGowan and Smith, 1978; Papanek,

1973; Ray and Webster, 1978; Rubinson, 1976; Stoneman, 1975; Szymanski, 1976).

Despite this attention, there are deficiencies in previous works which make further investigation of the relationship between dependency and growth a necessity. For example, Christopher Chase-Dunn (1975) and Albert Szymanski (1976) only investigate growth in the manufacturing sector; they ignore overall growth. This tactic is insufficient for understanding growth due to the possibility that overall economic growth could be robust without growth in the manufacturing sector. In the post-industrialized developed world, this scenario may in fact be the norm due to the decline of manufacturing sectors in relation to service sectors.

Szymanski (1976) produced a cross-national study of Latin American countries covering the time period from 1960-72 including five measures of aid and direct foreign investment as indicators of dependency. Szymanski concludes that dependency is related to high rates of profit repatriation, a finding which is consistent with dependency theory. Unfortunately, Szymanski fails to investigate how that profit repatriation affected growth, inequality, or physical quality of life in Latin America. Hence, Szymanski cannot rule out that dependency may have had a myriad of beneficial effects for Latin America in spite of the profit repatriation.

A number of studies (Kaufman et al., 1975; Papanek, 1973; Ray and Webster, 1978; Stoneman, 1975) investigate growth in GNP instead of GNP per capita growth. The selection of GNP growth as the dependent variable in these studies is somewhat problematic. Since a population growth which outstrips GNP growth depresses overall GNP per capita, the importance of the conclusions reached in these studies becomes questionable.

Patrick McGowan and Dale Smith (1980) offer a more sophisticated analysis in their study of economic dependency in black Africa. McGowan and Smith distinguish between economic power dependency and economic market dependency. Economic power dependency is a type of dependency which results from the underdeveloped nature of the LDC economy itself. Economic market dependency is a type of dependency which results from economic reliance upon the international market for goods, services, capital and technology. Economic power dependency is measured through four variables: the percentage of aid coming from the major donor in 1967, the percentage of exports going to the most important trading partner in 1967, the percentage of direct foreign investment coming from the major investing country in 1967, and the proportion of manufactured products among all exports between 1961 and 1963. Market dependency is measured by four variables: the three leading commodity exports as a percentage of total exports in 1967, trade as a percentage of GNP in 1965, direct foreign investment per capita in 1967, and total direct foreign investment in 1967. These variables were then correlated with 23 variables representing differing aspects of economic performance. The results achieved by McGowan and Smith were generally unsupportive of the dependency contention that dependency stunts growth; however, McGowan and Smith's work, though useful, suffers from several deficiencies, some of which will be discussed in the following section.

First, McGowan and Smith are unable to fully tap aid dependency since their measure taps only the largest donor rather than all aid from the core. Second, trade as a percentage of GNP does not separate trade with the core from trade with the periphery; therefore, this variable may be tapping a great deal of interdependence as well as dependence. Third, total direct foreign investment may be highly correlated with GNP, thus measuring the actual size of the economy rather than dependency. Additionally, the time frame of analysis is insufficient for the inference of causal relationships, and the sample of "black Africa" alone is not necessarily generalizable to all LDCs. Finally, McGowan and Smith do not introduce sufficient control variables such as level of wealth, area, and population size which may be very important factors of economic development.

In addition to these area studies, such as McGowan and Smith's, numerous cross-national studies which transcend geographic regional constraints have been completed on the impact of dependency on growth and inequality in LDCs. Among the earliest important efforts is the work of Johan Galtung (1971). Galtung measures dependency as the ratio of raw material exports and manufactured imports to total exports and imports, trade partner concentration as a percentage of total exports, and the percentage of exports which consist of the three most important commodities. Galtung correlates these indices with GNP per capita and finds that dependency negatively correlates with GNP per capita. This result is problematic as an indicator of the dependency/development relationship since it does not tap the relationship of dependency with growth. Essentially, Galtung's analysis can offer no insight into whether dependency may tend to increase or decrease the underdeveloped nature of economies in LDCs over time. Additionally, Galtung's sample includes both core and periphery nations which might obscure the patterns observable among LDCs alone. Galtung also ignores several important aspects of dependency such as direct foreign investment, debt dependency, and aid dependency.

David Rapkin (1976) improves on the work of Galtung by utilizing economic growth as his dependent variable and finds a negative relationship between economic growth and reliance on primary products as exports, commodity concentration, and exports to the single largest destination as a proportion of total exports. However, Rapkin fails to control for wealth, population size, or area, all of which may have important consequences for economic growth, and he ignores direct foreign investment, aid, and debt as dependency indicators.

Robert Jackman (1982) investigates the impact of foreign investment on growth in LDCs for the years 1967 and 1973. Jackman utilizes direct foreign investment for the years 1967 and 1973 as the independent variables, and the annual percentage growth rate in GNP per capita from 1960-1978 as the dependent variable. Jackman includes controls for GNP, population size, and changes in birth rates for 72 countries. Jackman finds that foreign investment has an insignificant impact on growth in LDCs and is thus unsupportive of the dependency perspective; however, Jackman did not measure dependency per se, but only one aspect of dependency, foreign investment. Jackman also failed to control for area, possibly a significant factor impacting dependency since countries with very small geographic area are unlikely to be self sufficient in most economic and natural resource areas. Finally, Jackman's foreign investment figures for 1967 could not have affected growth from the years 1960-66, raising questions of validity due to time sequencing. Despite these problems, Jackman's contribution should be considered noteworthy since he is one of the few scholars who controlled for significant internal factors, such as population size.

In general, the conclusions based on the empirical analysis have tended to support the dependency position that dependency is negatively associated with economic growth. The methodological problems which are present in the literature, however, are sufficient to merit questioning of the results. Perhaps most importantly, the figures used for dependency tended to be cross-sectional in character, and therefore, unable to provide much insight into causation. Consequently, we argue for further investigation of the relationship between dependency and economic growth.

Dependency and Inequality

Empirical studies dealing with income inequality have tended to show that dependency has a positive relationship with inequality. A number of studies (Bornschier, 1975, 1978; Chase-Dunn, 1975; Kaufman et al., 1975; and Rubinson, 1976) conclude that investment dependence is positively associated with inequality. Some of these studies (Chase-Dunn, 1975; Rubinson, 1976; Chase-Dunn and Rubinson, 1978; Bornschier et al., 1978) also conclude that aid dependency is positively related to inequality. Consequently, one would expect that the relationship between aid and investment dependency and inequality has been well established; however, as Bornschier et al. (1978, p. 664) admit, all of these studies have been cross-sectional because data sufficient for longitudinal analysis on inequality have not been available. In the words of Bornschier et al. (1978, p. 665):

> It is possible, therefore, to also argue that countries with more
> unequal income distributions attract more foreign investment and aid
> and that inequality and dependence form a mutually reinforcing
> pattern.

In a study which was longitudinal in character, Atul Kohli et al. (1984) investigate the relationship between penetration by multinational corporations and inequality. Kohli et al. find that both economic development and foreign investment are associated with increased inequality in cross-sectional analysis of 1970 data; however, in the ensuing longitudinal analysis, they find no relationship between penetration by multinational corporations and inequality. John Ravenhill (1986), however, criticizes Kohli et al. for methodological errors citing too short a time period and the removal of outliers or deviant cases from the analysis which did not fit their conclusions.

William Tyler and Peter Wogart (1973) measure dependency as the ratio of foreign trade to GNP, the percentage of total exports represented by the two major commodities, and the ratio of exports going to the two largest trade partners to total exports. As a dependent variable, Tyler and Wogart used the percentage of national income received by the poorest twenty percent, poorest sixty percent, and wealthiest five percent of the population. Tyler and Wogart's results supported the predictions of dependency theorists in that the share of national income going to the wealthiest five percent was positively related to their measures of dependency. However, no control variables were introduced into their bivariate regressions and this, coupled with the fact that their nine regressions were unable to produce an R2 over .20, suggests that factors other than dependency explain the largest percentage of the variance in inequality.

Among the most important area studies is the work of Robert Kaufman, Harry Chernotsky, and David Geller (1975) on Latin America. Kaufman et al. utilize four variables for trade dependency and four variables for capital dependency and correlate them with measures of inequality and growth rates. Kaufman et al. find income inequality to be positively related to economic dependency as dependency advocates would expect, but they also find that growth is positively related to inequality. Therefore, inequality may be generated by capitalist growth, not dependency; however, data on independent variables utilized by Kaufman et al. were for one year only (1967); therefore, no causal inferences can be drawn and the effects of dependency over time cannot be analyzed. Furthermore, it is questionable if relationships discovered in Latin America can be generalized to all LDCs.

Christopher Chase-Dunn and Richard Rubinson (1978) perform a cross-national empirical analysis of dependency, growth, and inequality. For economic dependency, Chase-Dunn and Rubinson use the following variables: the log of average 1950-55 profits earned by foreign investment in the host country, and total external public debt in 1965. Chase-Dunn and Rubinson's analysis omits any measures of trade dependency, aid dependency, technological dependency, or unequal exchange, focusing only on investment dependency. Curiously, direct foreign investment is not utilized as an indicator of investment dependence. Economic development was measured by the log of GNP per capita in 1950 and 1970, the log of electricity consumed per capita in 1950 and 1965, and the percentage of non-agricultural male labor force in 1950 and 1960. Income inequality was measured by Felix Paukert's (1973) Gini index for only one year, 1965. As a control variable, Chase-Dunn and Rubinson utilize domestic capital formation. They find that economic development is negatively related to the profits earned by foreign investment as well as external public debt. They also find that both independent variables were positively related to inequality. However, Chase-Dunn's analysis is weak in a longitudinal sense since the only year used for inequality was 1965 and only two years were used in investigating economic development. Additionally, growth was not controlled for when testing for inequality; therefore, growth can not be excluded as the cause for the inequality instead of dependency.

Bornschier, Chase-Dunn, and Rubinson (1978) analyze the effect of direct foreign investment and aid flows on income inequalities in LDCs and economic development. Their analysis is a test only of the aid and investment aspects of dependency, once again omitting measures of trade dependency, technological dependency, and unequal exchange. They distinguish between two types of MNC penetration: stocks and flows. Stocks include the total amount of accumulated foreign capital in a country and flows describe the amount of foreign capital coming into a country within a limited time period. For their analysis, Bornschier et al. utilize the figures on stocks and flows from 1967 only. They include in their sample 76 LDCs, omitting the most highly developed and the socialist states. As dependent variables, Bornschier et al. use the GNP per capita growth rates from 1960-1975. The results were that the effects of foreign capital were negative with growth in all regions of LDCs and most negative among wealthier states. They also observed differences in the impact of stocks and flows of foreign investment, with flows increasing growth in the short term, but stocks having a long term negative effect, but their research suggested that both direct foreign investment and aid increase inequality.

Though the work of Bornschier et al. is widely recognized, the design utilized by Bornschier et al. is somewhat problematic. The inclusion of direct foreign investment figures for only one year in the analysis presents problems for the same reasons that the usage of inequality figures for only one year presents problems as admitted by Bornschier et al. Essentially, the direction of the causal arrow is impossible to determine if figures are used for only one year. Additionally, the measuring of direct foreign investment for one year only presents even greater problems due to the volatile nature of the variable itself. Direct foreign investment in LDCs is often subject to wide swings from massive amounts of investment as a percentage of GNP in some years, to none in others. Political changes, such as nationalization of extractive mineral industries, political unrest, or currency instability may have huge effects on direct foreign investment from year to year. Furthermore, small states with small economies may experience huge short-term increases in direct foreign investment as percentages of GNP as the result of one or a few short-term projects and then return to very little direct foreign investment when the projects are completed. We argue that due to this volatile nature of the direct foreign investment variable, studies which investigate investment dependence based on investment for one year must be viewed with a high degree of skepticism.

Volker Bornschier and Thanh-Huyen Ballmer-Cao (1979) investigate the relationship between MNC penetration and inequality, controlling for GNP. Bornschier and Ballmer-Cao employ a path analysis in order to show that the direct effects of penetration by multinational corporations on inequality are slight, but the indirect effects are substantial. Bornschier and Ballmer-Cao use strength of organized labor as an intervening variable between multinational penetration and inequality. The cross-sectional character of this research is (admittedly) unable to rule out the possibility that the causal arrow runs in the opposite direction. In other words, multinational penetration may be weak in countries with strong organized labor due to its presence before the penetration. Thus the possibility remains that internal factors may be more responsible for equality than external factors, contrary to the tenets of dependency theory. The research also suffers from the previously mentioned problems surrounding the measurement of foreign investment for only one year.

Volker Bornschier (1981) again investigates the relationship between MNC penetration and both growth and inequality, this time controlling for the size of the economy, and finds that penetration by MNCs over the short-term produces growth, but the long-term effects are slower growth. Furthermore, penetration is observed to be positively related to inequality and accounts for 53 percent of the variance in inequality. Bornschier also finds that MNC penetration produces more inequality in all economic sectors except for agriculture. Once again, however, the research design is somewhat problematic. MNC penetration is again measured through direct foreign investment for only one year, 1967; however, Bornschier (1981, p. 385) adds to the design a variable which he labels "MNC fresh investment" from 1967 to 1973 which he defines as the "change in the total stock of foreign direct investment related to the GDP." Bornschier considers this variable useful for tapping the "short term effects" of MNC penetration; however, he still considers direct foreign investment for 1967 to capture the "long term effects" of MNC penetration.

The work of Bornschier et al. (1978) is in part contradicted by Michael Dolan and Brian Tomlin (1980). Dolan and Tomlin use the same measures of direct foreign investment for the same years as Bornschier et al. (1978), Bornschier and Ballmer Cao (1979), and Bornschier (1981). Like Bornschier et al., Dolan and Tomlin's analysis revealed differences between stocks and flows of MNC penetration and similar relationships between stocks, flows, and growth to those observed by Bornschier et al. Regarding inequality, however, Dolan and Tomlin find MNC penetration to be negatively related to income inequality measured by the ratio of the income of the highest 20 percent of the population over the lowest 40 percent. Additionally, Dolan and Tomlin observe no significant effect of trade, aid, partner, and commodity concentrations on inequality.

Taking a somewhat different approach, Peter Evans and Michael Timberlake (1980) hypothesize that direct foreign investment produces inequality indirectly through marginalization of workers in LDCs and increasing unemployment in the tertiary sector. In a cross-national analysis, Evans and Timberlake use direct foreign investment in 1967 as an independent variable and control for GDP, regressing the variables on seven measures of inequality. Evans and Timberlake also regress the independent variables on changes in tertiary unemployment for the years 1950-1960 and find that investment dependency is positively related to both inequality and employment in the tertiary sector. Evans and Timerlake's work suffers from the same problems as other scholars, such as Bornschier et al. (1978), in that direct foreign investment is measured through figures for 1967 only. Furthermore, the time sequential ordering appears to be suspect since it would be difficult for direct foreign investment in 1967 to impact inequality and employment in the 1950s and 1960.

Other Empirical Studies

In addition to the empirical analyses of the relationships between dependency and growth or inequality, there are a number of other important works which are relevant to the purposes here. A few of those studies are given space below.

Lynn Mytelka (1980) explores the concept of technological dependency in the Andean countries of Latin America. Mytelka operationalized technological dependency through survey data of Latin American executives who offered their judgment whether their firms could produce their own technology for new products. Mytelka found a high correlation between previous licensing agreements and the inability to develop new technology, suggesting that direct foreign investment and licensing agreements had little technology spillover effects. Mytelka argues that licensing agreements with foreign firms for technology reduce domestic research and development incentives. Mytelka did not, however, tie technological dependence to sluggish growth or inequality.

Several studies which investigate dependency relationships are case studies which focus on one country. Perhaps atypical of these are the works of William Leolegrande (1979), Carmelo Mesa-Lago (1981), and Robert Packenham (1986), all of which investigate the effects of dependency on Cuba. The purposes of these studies are to show that dependency can and does exist in socialist, as well as capitalistic, societies. These studies are also significant because dependency is measured through multiple variables and the scholars attempt to capture a more comprehensive essence of dependency instead of merely a certain element such as investment dependency or aid dependency. All three studies investigate trade dependency, aid dependency, export commodity concentration, and trade partner concentration as aspects of dependency. The conclusions of all three studies were that the transition to socialism in Cuba was unsuccessful in severing the bonds of dependency.

Steven Jackson (1979) offers a research design which could be utilized for dependency analysis. Jackson argues that dependency should be measured through the level of import of capital goods, the percentage of imports of machinery and transport equipment of total imports, private foreign investment, external public debt, and patent and trademark registration figures to assess the extent of foreign penetration in LDCs. Jackson argues that scholars should control for the size of the peripheral economy through the use of GNP. Jackson analyzes data for the years 1965 and 1970 for twenty-four diverse LDCs for the purpose of assessing the extent of dependency in LDCs. Jackson finds a great deal of variation in his measures of penetration of LDCs, suggesting that there indeed are degrees of dependency and that dependency should not be categorized as a dichotomy. Jackson does not, however, assess the effects of the penetration on growth or inequality.

In sum, the above studies are, perhaps, only the tip of the iceberg of literature empirically investigating the relationship between growth, inequality, and dependency. The empirical studies investigating dependency are extremely diverse in character. Alschuler (1976), Evans (1972), Kaufman, Chernotsky, and Geller (1975), and Szymanski (1976) focus only on Latin America. McGowan and Smith (1978) focus only on Africa. Some authors (Kaufman et al., 1975; Rubinson, 1977) exclude oil states from their analysis. Socialist countries are generally excluded from the analysis. The data gathered for analysis tend to be from the 1950-1970 period. Bornschier et al. (1978), Bornschier and Ballmer-Cao (1978), Kaufman et al. (1975), Papanek (1973), Szymanski (1976), Chase-Dunn (1975), Rubinson (1976), and Bornschier (1981) all measure investment dependence. Szymanski (1976), Chase-Dunn (1975), and Rubinson (1976) all include measures of aid dependence. Alschuler (1976) measures trade dependence.

In general, independent variables employed tend to tap direct foreign investment, aid, debt, unequal exchange, trade dependency, commodity concentration, and trade partner concentration as components of dependency. Technological dependency and energy dependency are generally ignored. As far as control variables are concerned, Chase-Dunn (1975) and Rubinson (1976) control for the amount of mineral resources, including oil. Bornschier and Ballmer-Cao (1978) and Chase-Dunn (1975) control for domestic capital formation, the former group also controls for population growth. Numerous studies (Kaufman et al., 1975; Stevenson, 1972; Szymanski, 1976; and McGowan and Smith, 1978), however, do not include any control variables at all. For dependent variables, changes in GNP per capita is most often used to estimate growth (Bornschier et al., 1978). Similarly, the most often used measure of income inequality is personal income inequality either measured by the Gini Index or some other ratio of income inequality between a wealthy top percentage of the population and poorer population segments (Bornschier et al., 1978).

Overall, the results of these dependency studies have been mixed. There appears to be a lack of consensus on the relationship between dependency and growth and dependency and inequality; however, Bornschier's (1981) review of the literature suggests that studies have generally been supportive of a positive relationship between inequality and penetration by multinational corporations. We argue that this consensus has been based on insufficient data since inequality and direct foreign investment figures utilized in the analysis tended to represent only one year. The hypotheses and variables which will be utilized in this project will be discussed in the following chapter.

Chapter 4

Methods and Data

Hypotheses

In the following section, the possibilities and expectations surrounding the empirical investigation of dependency are explored as well as some of the problems inherent in investigating dependency. The basic hypotheses of this research and the logic underlying these hypotheses are also introduced and discussed.

In general, the term "dependency" is interpreted here in a manner consistent with the interpretation of Richard Rubinson (1977, p. 5) who argues that dependency refers to "the degree to which a country is subject to economic factors controlled by foreign actors." Used in this manner, dependency is a variable feature of relationships among states and its effects are subject to empirical investigation.

There are numerous possible relationships between dependency and the dependent variables. To begin with, it is most likely that dependency explains some, but certainly nowhere near all, of the variance in economic development among LDCs. In other words, development or underdevelopment may be partly due to dependency and partly due to factors other than dependency which are unaccounted for by dependency theorists. This probability produces difficulties for the researcher in interpretation of the results. Essentially, what percentage of the variance must dependency explain in order for it to be considered "supported" by the results? Any answer to this question must be somewhat subjective; however, we argue that dependency must surely be found to account for at least ten percent of the variance for it to be considered supported even in the mildest sense. As strong and deterministic as the language is in some of the dependency literature (as was revealed previously in the review of the literature), it is not without basis to argue that dependency theory would require dependency to explain the majority of the variance in the development variables (although we do not argue that dependency must produce such strong relationships in order to be supported).

A second major problem in the interpretation of the results of the analysis is that there may be spurious causes of changes in both the dependency indicators and the dependent variables which are unrelated to the relationship between dependency and development, yet nonetheless produce covariation. For example, natural disasters, such as floods or earthquakes, may have serious deleterious effects on PQLI in an LDC and be the main cause of lower PQLI during a time period which coincidentally witnessed increased dependency.

Therefore, it is with great care that the results must be interpreted and without 100 percent positive conclusions that the results will be presented.

Dependency may have positive, negative, mixed, or no relationship with each dependent variable when controls are taken into account. The variables which are selected to represent dependency may easily prove to be multidirectional in character with different aspects of dependency producing both positive and negative relationships with each dependent variable. In such a case, interpretation of the findings becomes more difficult; however, such a scenario is not predicted by dependency theory; therefore, directionally mixed findings remain important as results which are unsupportive of dependency theory.

Dependency may prove to be negatively related to GNP per capita, yet positively related to GNP per capita growth. A negative relationship with GNP per capita would be predicted by dependency theory; however, a simultaneous positive relationship between GNP per capita growth and dependency would suggest that the negative relationship between GNP per capita and dependency is not a causal relationship in the direction espoused by dependency theory. In other words, the logical conclusion would be that dependency is a characteristic of states with lower GNP per capita, but not a factor which tends to depress GNP per capita growth and produce further "underdevelopment." This scenario is essentially what is expected to be discovered in this analysis. We expect dependency to be negatively associated with GNP per capita; the possibility that states with lower GNPs per capita would be more dependent makes sound logical sense. However, we argue that it is not dependency which produced the lower GNP per capita, but that dependency is merely a characteristic of states with lower GNP per capita and not a factor which perpetuates or depresses GNP per capita. This statement can essentially be supported if dependency is unrelated or positively associated with GNP per capita growth. We hypothesize that dependency is positively related to GNP per capita growth.

This hypothesis essentially has as its basis the liberal paradigm which views increased trade and contact between the core and periphery as beneficial for both. Much of what are viewed as components of the overall concept of dependency (aid, debt, direct foreign investment, high trade volume and trade partner concentration) are viewed as beneficial to economic growth by liberal theorists. The hypothesis is also based on the observation that the newly industrialized countries of Asia (South Korea, Taiwan, Singapore, Hong Kong) achieved their economic leaps during a period of increased relationships with the core. Simultaneously, many of the least developed states such as Ethiopia and Somalia have had comparatively less contact with the core.

While it is expected that dependency will exhibit a positive relationship with growth, it is possible that it may simultaneously exhibit no relationship with inequality, neither of which would be predicted by dependency advocates. It is possible that the positive relationship discovered by a number of scholars between MNC penetration and inequality is spurious and that the real relationship is between growth and inequality. It is also highly probable that any inequality which is produced through foreign investment may be offset through aid, despite the arguments of Bornschier (1981) to the contrary.

We argue that it is not dependency which produces inequality, but rather other factors within LDCs that are not accounted for by dependency such as rapid population growth and high rates of GNP per capita growth. This argument is based upon the findings of Abbas Pourgerami (1991) and Samuel Huntington and Joan Nelson (1976) who respectively found greater inequality in authoritarian regimes and a growth/equity trade-off. The argument that dependency is unrelated to inequality is also consistent with the findings of Dolan and Tomlin (1980) who are unable to find a dependency/inequality linkage. We hypothesize that there is no significant relationship between dependency and inequality when controls are included for population growth, GNP per capita growth, and regime type. Based upon the works of Pourgerami, Dolan and Tomlin, and Huntington and Nelson, we expect that dependency may not explain a significant portion of the variance in inequality.

Although at odds with dependency theory, this hypothesis is also inconsistent with the liberal paradigm which tends to view core contact and growth as factors which tend to reduce inequalities. It should be mentioned, however, that the liberal paradigm assumes that contact with the core increases domestic investment through addition rather than merely displacing domestic investment and limiting the opportunities of domestic capital. The liberal paradigm also assumes that the demand for labor is not skewed toward the skilled worker (Cline, 1975, p. 372). Intuitively, we do not expect these assumptions to be satisfied in LDCs since it is only reasonable that direct foreign investment and trade with the core would limit some opportunities for domestic capital investment. Hence, dependency, which increases under the liberal paradigm, may not reduce inequalities.

Additionally, we expect to find a positive relationship between dependency and the growth of the physical quality of life index (PQLI) in LDCs. This hypothesis is based on the assumption that greater contact with the core, especially in the form of aid (Snider, 1971), brings modern medical, educational, and sanitary supplies and technology to LDCs applying upward pressure to the PQLI. While it is possible that dependency may be negatively related to PQLI in LDCs, we argue that if this is the case, the association is not causal in character, and the spurious nature of the relationship can be shown if dependency does not also exhibit a negative association with the growth of PQLI (Quality Improvement). If such is the case, the inference which may be drawn is that dependency is a characteristic of states with low PQLIs, but not a factor which acts to perpetuate lower PQLIs.

Essentially, we do not dispute the position of dependency theorists that dependency does indeed exist, nor that LDCs are often economically dependent on developed western states, nor that the elites in LDCs may often have interests very much in common with those of the more developed West. Rather, we argue that the greater the degree of this dependency, the greater the development in LDCs in terms of GNP per capita growth and PQLI growth.

Finally, we argue that clientelism (as described by Galtung, 1971) has a positive effect on the physical quality of life in LDCs. Although dependency theorists may be correct in their assertion that interests of elites in the periphery often become consistent with the interests of elites in the core, it does not follow that the physical quality of life in LDCs will diminish due to this clientelism. On the contrary, the stronger this clientelism, the more likely that the physical quality of life in LDCs will rise since it is in the interest of core elites to keep the masses of workers alive and healthy in order to take advantage of their labor. Secondly, dependency theorists seem to completely discard all of the humanitarian and philanthropic efforts of core countries which can only be expected to be greatest when clientelism is highest. In order to clarify, the three basic hypotheses of this project are repeated below:

Hypothesis 1. Dependency is positively related to GNP per capita growth in LDCs.
Hypothesis 2. Dependency is unrelated to inequality in LDCs.
Hypothesis 3. Dependency is positively related to growth in the physical quality of life in LDCs.

Independent Variables: Dependency

In this section the independent variables which represent dependency will be introduced and the logic behind their selection as dependency indicators will be discussed. The basic set of indicators which are introduced are intended to represent a broad range of phenomena which are the nearest feasible representation of dependency.

Dependency theorists argue that the dependent relationships between the core states and the periphery are complex and dynamic. Therefore, there is no single economic relationship but a wide range of economic relationships which constitute dependency. In the words of Jeanne Gobalet and Larry J. Diamond (1979, p. 414),

> Dependency is a comprehensive condition of national subordination, pervading the economic, political, and social structure, in which the entire framework of the dependent nation is conditioned by the needs, actions and interests of other and dominant nations.

Several variables will thus be employed to analyze this dynamic and complex phenomenon which has been labeled as dependency. Guillermo O'Donnell (1973) argues that scholars should focus on the portion of the economies in LDCs which become integrated into the world economy. In this sense, dependency theorists are unconcerned with economic segments which remain uncapitalized, such as subsistence farming. It is the assumption of dependency theorists that the integration of core economies with peripheral economies is qualitatively different than the integration which transpires between core economies in that the core-periphery economic integration is asymmetric in character (Jackson, 1979). Consequently, the indicators which will be utilized to represent dependency must be indicators which tap into this asymmetric nature of core-periphery relations.

There are numerous ways that economies in LDCs may become asymmetrically integrated into the world economy. In the following section, indicators will be presented which are intended to tap this asymmetrical integration. The first of these elements, which will be presented here as an indicator of dependency, is what Philippe Schmitter (1971) terms as "trade dependency."

Trade Dependency

In an early empirical investigation of the dependency paradigm, Schmitter (1971) engaged in analysis of the dependency perspective for the purpose of discovering how well the paradigm applied to LDCs in Latin America. Schmitter employed a cross-sectional design involving twenty Latin American states and 102 variables based upon aggregate socioeconomic and political data. Schmitter performed a factor analysis of the variables which produced three factors labeled as external dependency. One of Schimitter's dependency factors was trade dependency. Schmitter found trade dependency to exert a negative impact on economic growth in LDCs. Schmitter's work is typical of the empirical literature on dependency where trade with the core by LDCs is widely recognized as an important aspect of dependency.

Similar to Schmitter in that he views trade with the core as a variable which taps an aspect of dependency, Carmelo Mesa-Lago (1981, p. 79) argues that

> the more a country relies on foreign trade to obtain goods and services that are not produced domestically and the larger and more dominant the external export sector is, the more vulnerable the economy of the country may become to external forces.

Similarly, Leolegrande (1979, p. 5) argues that international trade is one of the foremost mechanisms, and therefore indicators, of dependency. Robert Packenham (1986, p. 62), who also measures dependency, concurs with Mesa-Lago and Leolegrande, arguing that "the larger the trade sector in relation to total economic activity, the more dependent the country's economy."

The implications are clear. Trade volume as a percentage of a state's economy should be considered to be an integral part of dependency. The higher the volume of trade as a percentage of GNP, the greater the dependency. Theoretically, if an LDC has a high volume of trade as a percentage of GNP, then its prosperity and growth should be inexorably linked to "international economic and political events over which no domestic economic or political actors can exert any substantial degree of control" as outlined by Chilcote and Edelstein (1974).

Trade dependency, however, must be qualified by separating trade with the core from trade with the periphery. Essentially, dependency theorists such as Frank (1967) do not view trade between LDCs as harmful, but only view trade with the core as having detrimental effects. Consequently, trade dependency in this study will be measured as the percentage of total trade as a percentage of GNP of each LDC with states listed among the category of "high income countries" by the World Bank. Other scholars who have utilized trade volume with the core as a measure of trade dependency include Kaufman et al. (1975), Bornschier and Balmer Cao (1979), Rubinson (1977), Bornschier (1981), and McGowan and Smith (1980).

Trade Partner Concentration

Trade partner concentration is the percentage of trade volume which a state may transact with one (or possibly two) trading partners. Scholars argue that when trade is concentrated in one or a very few partners, states become dependent (Leolegrande, 1979, p. 12; Packenham, 1990, p. 63; Mesa-Lago, 1981, p. 92). In the words of Dolan and Tomlin (1980, 43), "dependency concerns not only the absolute levels of trade, but also the concentration of these linkages." Some form of trade partner concentration is also utilized as an indicator of dependency by Dolan and Tomlin (1980), McGowan and Smith (1980), and Bornschier et al. (1978), Rubinson (1977), and Galtung (1971). According to Leolegrande (1979, p. 12), trade partner concentration renders states not only dependent economically on a very few states, but also renders them dependent on political forces within the principal trading partner. In other words, political decisions within the principal trading partner to raise tariffs, impose economic sanctions, embargoes, or boycotts are decisions outside of the control of the LDC, and therefore, enhance their dependence. Leolegrande vividly illustrates this point by illuminating the effect of the US trade boycott, which was employed against Cuba following the socialist revolution, on the Cuban economy.

High trade partner concentration not only renders states more vulnerable to the disruptions of a trade boycott by the principal trading partner, but also increases the likelihood of detrimental effects from changes in tariffs, changes in import-export patterns, fluctuations in the principal trade partner's economy, or fluctuations in the exchange rates in the principal trade partner. Furthermore, principal trade partners for many LDCs are likely to be core states, principally the United States, the very metropolis which Frank argues hinders growth through exploitive relationships with the periphery. Trade concentrated in one or a few partners should exacerbate the possibility that the "prosperity and growth of a dependent economy is a function of international economic and political events over which no domestic economic or political actors can exert any substantial degree of control" (Chilcote and Edelstein, 1974, p. 34). Therefore, trade partner concentration is accepted here as a valid indicator of dependency. However, in order to insure that the core-periphery relationship is tapped, if the major trading partner of an LDC is another LDC, then that trade partner will be excluded from the analysis. Trade partner concentration will, therefore, be measured for each LDC as the percentage of overall trade volume accounted for by the largest two core country trading partners. Once again, the designation of a state as a core country will be dictated by the World Bank categorization of states as high-income.

Dependence on Nonfuel Primary Products in Exports

Dependency theorists also point to dependence on nonfuel primary products in economic exports as an indicator of part of an "unequal exchange" relationship in trade, fostering underdevelopment, transfer of capital to the core, and dependency (Prebisch, 1971; Bath and James, 1976). Obviously, the greater percentage of a state's economy dependent on one or a few primary product exports, the greater the dependency of that state on external factors affecting demand and prices. A world market glut of the one product, which makes up a large percentage of a state's exports, may send the state's economy into a downward spiral due to low prices and a drop in exports despite the capacity of the state to increase production on a steady basis. In other words, reliance on nonfuel primary products in exports makes it easier for external factors to influence local economies. To exacerbate the effect further, dependency theorists (Prebisch, 1973) argue that raw material prices (other than oil) tend to rise at a much slower rate than the prices of manufactured goods, therefore placing dependent states at a long-term disadvantage in terms of trade. Furthermore, Mesa-Lago (1981, p. 216) attributes the robust economies of Singapore, Taiwan, and South Korea to diversification in exports, offsetting the fact that all three states are heavily dependent on foreign trade, imports, and exports. Scholars who include reliance on raw materials in exports as a variable in measuring for dependency include Mesa-Lago (1981) and McGowan and Smith (1980). For the purposes of this study, reliance on nonfuel primary products in exports, measured as the nonfuel primary products percentage of total exports, will be utilized as an indicator of dependency, consistent with Bath and James (1976) proposition #2(a).

Debt Dependency

Much attention has been given over the last twenty years both in scholarly works and in the news media to the effects of Third World debt on development. To paraphrase Ronald Chilcote and Joel Edelstein (1974), external debt burdens are but one of the "variety of mechanisms" through which resources are siphoned from LDCs by the core. Obviously, exorbitant debt service diverts resources from more productive enterprises and may become an inhibitor to development. Furthermore, scholars argue that the greater the external debt, the more states become dependent on external forces (especially through the restrictions placed on loans by creditors and governments in the core) and therefore subject to greater leverage and constraints imposed upon their economies by the core. (Prebisch, 1961; Futardo, 1972; Payer, 1974; Rubinson, 1977).

Dependency theorists contend that the lending practices of international lending institutions, which include placing contingencies on borrowing by linking loans to economic reforms within LDCs, erode the sovereignty of the borrowing states and reduce their ability to make autonomous political-economic decisions (Donaldson, 1991, 155). The conditions of loans often include currency devaluations, agreements to remove tariff restraints, deregulation of economic controls, and the reduction of deficits (Donaldson, 1991, 155). The effects of such conditions obviously place some control over the domestic policies of LDCs in the hands of the world's lending institutions. Joan Spero (1990, 147-158), in fact, places the responsibility for the original indebtedness of much of the Third World to ECLA import substitution policies and asserts that the indebtedness of oil producing LDCs such as Mexico can be, in large part, attributed to loans made under the presumption of lending institutions that oil would continue to be in short supply and prices would continue to exceed $30 per barrel.

Consequently, it is not surprising that scholars who measure dependency include external debt as an indicator of dependency (Mesa-Lago, 1981; Packenham, 1990; Leolegrande, 1979). Debt dependency falls well within both proposition #1 of Chilcote and Edelstein since debt leads to political and economic control of LDCs by external actors, and their proposition #2, since debt is a mechanism which results in a long-term net capital drain on the LDC, hindering sustained economic growth. Debt dependency will be measured as external debt as a percentage of GNP.

Energy Dependency

The oil shocks of the 1970's illustrated the economic ramifications of energy dependency even for the most developed states such as the United States, much less the economies of LDCs. A reliable supply of adequate energy is, perhaps, invaluable to industrialization and economic development. Frequently, some measure of energy or energy production is used by scholars as an indicator of economic development (Packenham, 1979). To the extent that states depend on external sources for energy, their economies are more or less dependent, and development may depend on external sources. Consequently, it is not surprising that scholars who have measured dependency have tended to include energy dependence in their measurements (Mesa-Lago, 1981; Packenham, 1979). Energy dependency obviously falls within the bounds of proposition #1 as a situation over which domestic actors in LDCs cannot exert any substantial control. Energy production as a percentage of consumption will be utilized as an indicator of energy dependency. With the use of this indicator, energy dependency increases as energy production as a percentage of consumption decreases.

Direct Foreign Investment

Dos Santos (1970), Cardoso and Faletto (1979), and Evans (1979) argue that the investment by multinational corporations (MNCs) in LDCs constitutes a "new dependency." Although this aspect of dependency may be labeled "new dependency," it is most certainly not new. The proposition that direct foreign investment by the core in LDCs constitutes a component of dependency appears to have wide acceptance among dependency scholars. For example, Amin (1976, p. 287) argues that contact with MNCs works to drain capital from LDCs. Stoneman (1975) and Duvall (1978) argue that the most critical aspect of dependency is foreign ownership and control of domestic capital stock. In Schmitter's (1971) factor analysis involving 102 variables for Latin American countries, direct foreign investment emerged as one of the factors which he labeled as external dependence. Denis O'Hearn (1989, p. 578), in a process which is labeled "decapitalization," argued that penetration of TNCs into LDCs creates an outward flow of capital. In this view investment by TNCs in LDCs is directed at controlling the internal markets of underdeveloped countries, thereby rendering the LDCs more dependent. Bornschier and Chase-Dunn (1985, p. 51-52) argue that LDCs have become less dependent in terms of monoculture in exports and reliance on nonfuel primary products in exports, but that the former state of dependency has been supplanted by dependence on foreign investment and capital. Furthermore, dependency advocates such as Bruce London and Bruce Williams (1990, p. 570) argue that empirical studies which found no relationship between dependency and equity are flawed due to the omission of a measure of foreign investment.

As a consequence, a large number of scholars who have investigated dependency relationships advocate the inclusion of some form of core investment linkage as an indicator of dependency. Jackson (1979) argues that one strategy for measuring capitalist penetration into the periphery is to utilize the foreign domination of the supply of the capital stock. For this purpose, Jackson suggests utilization of "the extent to which the effective capital stock of a given peripheral economy has been supplied . . . . by the core of the global economy" (1979, p. 46). Other studies which utilize foreign direct investment as a measurement for dependency or core penetration include Stoneman (1975), Kaufman et al. (1975), Szymanski (1976), McGowan and Smith (1980), Dolan and Tomlin (1980), Bornschier et al. (1978), and Bornschier and Balmer-Cao (1979).

The basic assumption is that capital which has been asymmetrically supplied by the core influences the productive capacities of the host country in accordance with the wishes of the core. Therefore, in order to provide a remedy for the alleged trespasses of previous studies, direct foreign investment as a percentage of GNP will be included as an independent variable tapping one aspect of dependency. A large volume of foreign investment in relation to economic output is a factor in placing economic control outside of the host country and consistent with proposition #1 of Chilcote and Edelstein (1974).

Foreign Aid

Similar to the debt dependency argument, foreign external assistance to developing countries may provide the developed core with another mechanism through which LDCs can be externally controlled. Since the decisions of the core on whether or not to render aid are often political, tied to factors such as the ideological orientation of the LDC government or human rights (Wimberley, 1990, p. 76), underdeveloped states which desire to receive aid may be forced to comply with the wishes of the core in political orientation and the handling of dissidents. Consequently, an element of sovereignty could be eroded in the LDCs through the acceptance of foreign aid. Wimberley (1990, p. 76) also argues that foreign aid may provide a form of support for regimes which are unconcerned with the needs of the poor, thus contributing to continued inequity. Furthermore, Wimberley (1990, p. 76) argues that aid fosters "income inequality through promotion of capital-intensive, labor-conserving production where unemployment and underemployment are high." As a result, dependency theorists would expect aid to foster inequality. Schmitter (1971), in his factor analysis of 102 variables involving Latin American countries, observed that aid surfaced among his three factors which he labeled as external dependence.

Scholars who include aid variables in their analysis when investigating dependency relationships include Szymanski (1976), Dolan and Tomlin (1980), McGowan and Smith (1980), Leolegrande (1979), Mesa-Lago (1981), and Packenham (1990). Since whether or not LDCs may receive aid is a decision made within core states and dependent on politics outside of LDC control, foreign aid fits well within Chilcote and Edelstein's proposition #1 and Dos Santos' definition of dependency.

As explained by Jackson (1979), when investigating the impact of capitalist penetration through the usage of factors such as foreign aid, the size of the economy of the recipient country must be taken into account. Obviously, a ten million dollar aid receipt may have more impact on a very small economy such as Benin's than a very large economy such as that of Brazil. In such a case, the same ten million dollars, therefore, creates greater dependency in the smaller economy. If aid as a percentage of GNP is used instead of total development receipts, a truer picture of the degree of dependency created by the aid will be tapped. Consequently, for the purposes of this study, foreign aid dependence will be measured as average annual total development assistance receipts as a percentage of GNP.

Technological Independence

Technological dependency is a form of dependency stressed by Cardoso (1973). Cardoso argues that this form of dependency creates "functional derangement" or "functional incompleteness" of a national economy. In the words of Cardoso (1973, p. 163), capitalist accumulation in dependent economies does not complete its cycle. Lacking 'autonomous technology and compelled therefore to utilize imported technology, dependent capitalism is crippled.'

Technology dependence, according to Packenham (1990), may be of equal importance with other dependency variables such as direct foreign investment. Helge Hveem (1974) argues that productive knowledge plays a crucial role in the building of the "technocapital structure" of the world economy and is a necessary component for autonomous development. Jackson (1979) argues that coordination and control of the market is exercised largely through the exclusionary rights afforded by the possession of patents and trademarks. The primary role of patents and trademarks, according to M. Anandakrishnan and H. Morita-Lou (1988, p. 299), is to "encourage the disclosure of inventions for the benefit of the public at large in return for special compensation granted." Hence, patent data serve as "convenient tools" for the interpretation of technological status of a country since they record "almost all advances of technology" of a country as well as for those countries associated with that country.

The most important types of information which are available regarding patent data in developing counties are data concerning the number of patents granted in countries. According to Anandakrishnan and Morita-Lou (1988), the number of patents granted in a country can help reveal the nature of dependency and the extent of technological transfers in particular countries. If large numbers of domestic patents are granted within a country, then it is suggestive that that country is experiencing technological advancement. Conversely, countries within which no patents are granted are, therefore, dependent on other entities outside of their borders for technological advancement. Dependency theorists would expect a positive relationship between the number of domestic patents granted and growth, with fewer patents resulting in greater technological dependency and, therefore, slower growth. We argue that technological dependence can be captured through the number of domestic patents granted in LDCs. These data will be obtained from the World Intellectual Property Organization's *Industrial Property.*

The number of domestic patents granted is actually a measure of technological independence, rather than dependency. Consequently, dependency theorists would expect it to be positively related to all of the dependent variables utilized here. In this sense, liberals and dependency theorists appear to be in agreement since the liberal paradigm would also hold that technological independence would have a positive relationship with economic development. Despite this congruence between the two paradigms, we will include technological independence in the analysis in order to be fair to the dependency perspective.

Admittedly, the variables discussed above may not constitute an exhaustive list of indicators of dependency, but we argue that the above indicators taken together, if dependency theorists are correct, could explain a large portion of the variance in both growth and inequality. If these indicators are unable to explain a significant portion of the variance, contrary to the arguments of dependency theorists, then we argue that it is doubtful that any other indicators of dependency that could be added to the equation could explain more of the variance than the internal factors that dependency theorists tend to ignore.

Dependent Variables

In the following section, the dependent variables that are chosen for analysis are introduced and the rationale behind their selection is discussed. Included in the discussion of each variable is a discussion of its use in previous empirical studies.

Wealth

The most basic argument of the dependency perspective is, perhaps, the argument that dependency produces "underdevelopment." Underdevelopment may have numerous definitions, but among its most basic components it involves lower levels of wealth. GNP per capita is the most widely used indicator of level of wealth (Sofranko, Nolan, and Bealer, 1975). In order for dependency to produce underdevelopment, one would expect dependency to be associated with lower levels of GNP per capita.

A negative association of dependency with GNP per capita is certainly possible, if not probable, given the definition of dependency and the nature of the indicators selected here to reflect dependency. The dependency perspective itself was not created in a vacuum and must be based on some type of observations made by dependency scholars. What were observed by dependency scholars as characteristics of dependent states (such as reliance on raw material exports) may very well be general characteristics of states with lower levels of wealth or GNP per capita. Consequently, GNP per capita is included as a dependent variable in order to determine if dependency theorists are correct in their assertion that dependency is associated with states with lower levels of wealth.

If the results of the analysis do support the dependency perspective, this does not necessarily suggest that dependency perpetuates lower levels of wealth, but only that the two are associated. Hence, the possibility will remain open that the causal order may be reversed and dependency is the result of lower levels of wealth. In order to gain a clearer understanding of the causal order and determine whether dependency does indeed perpetuate lower levels of wealth, the relationship between dependency and GNP per capita growth must be investigated.

Growth

Development is a complex concept which lends itself to many diverse conceptualizations in scholarly literature, and therefore, perhaps also to complexity in measurement. As previously discussed, economic growth has been a primary concern of both dependency theorists and empirical analysis of dependency relationships.

There are numerous indicators that could be used to represent economic growth; however, according to Sofranko, Nolan, and Bealer (1975) in a rigorous analysis of indicators of economic development, there are several indicators often used to reflect development that are highly correlated. Additionally, Sofranko, Nolan and Bealer state that the most often used indicator of economic development is GNP per capita. Since dependency theory is concerned with development in terms of growth, annual percentage change in GNP per capita will be used to represent growth. Through the use of annual percentage change in GNP per capita, several advantages are gained. First, annual percentage change in GNP per capita is easily interpretable. Second, annual percentage change in GNP per capita introduces into the equation a measure that is somewhat relative in nature. The relative nature of growth is important, since dependent states theoretically, according to the radical dependency perspective, experience slower long term growth. Finally, GNP per capita growth appears to have wide acceptance as an indicator of economic growth since it has been utilized by a large number of scholars in analyzing dependency, including Bornschier (1975, 1981), Bornschier and Ballmer-Cao (1979), Dolan and Tomlin (1980), Gobalet and Diamond (1979), Jackman (1982), McGowan and Smith (1978), and Rubinson (1976).

In sum, the reasons for choosing GNP per capita growth over other indicators, such as Energy Consumption per capita, are threefold. First, data on GNP per capita growth are readily available from a host of reliable sources over a long period of time. Second, GNP per capita growth has been much more widely used by scholars who have empirically investigated dependency, and therefore, has a great amount of acceptance and familiarity. Third, in empirical tests, Sofranko, Nolan and Bealer (1975) found that GNP correlates highly with energy consumption per capita; therefore, if the two measures behave nearly the same, why complicate what could be robustly simplified by using a more complicated and less familiar measure?

Inequality

In testing for the validity of hypotheses espoused by dependency theorists, an alternate measure of development must be included, tapping an entirely different concept. According to Cardoso (in Bonilla and Girling, 1973, pp. 7-16), development is possible in dependent states, but not redistributive and benefits only the elites and international bourgeoisie. Similarly, Cockroft, Frank, and Johnson (1972, p. xv) argue that growth should not be confused with development and that growth without development is common. The inference of Cockroft, Frank, and Johnson is that development should be defined by equity, rather than economic growth. Similarly, Chilcote and Edelstein (1974, p. 28) argue that development in the dependency perspective should be defined as "equality, the elimination of alienation of the provision of meaningful work, and forms of social, economic and political organization which enable all members of society to determine the decisions which affect them." Chilcote and Edelstein (1974, p. 28) add that foreign penetration does bring an expanded GNP, but does not create self-sustaining development.

Obviously, the concept of development by dependency advocates is very different from what is tapped through the employment of GNP per capita or economic consumption per capita, and some dependency advocates do not dispute the hypothesis that these factors may rise with increased dependency. Instead, what is essentially argued is that dependency hinders the achievement of an equitable distribution of wealth within LDCs and that equity itself is the essence of development. Typical of such an approach is that of Norman Hicks and Paul Streeten (1979), who argue that there is a contradiction between economic growth and distribution of wealth, suggesting that dependency should be measured in terms of equity. In the words of Hicks and Streeten (1979, p. 577), "such a focus supplements attention to how much is being produced, by attention to what is being produced, in what ways, for whom and with what impact." Obviously, the inference is that economic growth itself should not be equated with development if large segments of the population fail to benefit from such growth.

We contend that the argument of dependency theorists that development is equal to equity is misguided (after all, using this criterion for development, the U.S. is no more developed than many states in the periphery); however, in order to challenge dependency theorists on their own terms, inequality will be measured in relation to the independent variables in this study in order to test the hypothesis that dependency fosters inequality as charged by dependency advocates.

A number of scholars who have investigated the relationship between inequality and dependency have utilized the Gini Index as an indicator of dependency (Bornschier, 1975, 1981; Bornschier and Ballmer-Cao, 1979; Chase-Dunn, 1975; Evans and Timberlake, 1980; Kaufman et al., 1975; Rubinson, 1976). Unfortunately, the Gini Index is not readily available in longitudinal data for all of the years necessary for this analysis. An alternative measure of inequality is offered by Dolan and Tomlin (1980), who utilize a ratio of inequality calculated from dividing the economic holdings of the top twenty percent of the population by the wealth of the bottom forty percent. Steve Chan and Cal Clark (1991) essentially follow the same tactic dividing the wealth of the top twenty percent of the population by the wealth of the bottom twenty percent of the population. Since the inequality data available from the World Bank are in quintiles, it makes sense that inequality should be measured utilizing the social inequity variable employed by Chan and Clark (1991), as the ratio between the income of the wealthiest twenty percent of the population and that of the poorest twenty percent. The higher the value for this variable, the greater the inequality.

Physical Quality of Life

Since the early 1970's, development strategies within international organizations have shifted somewhat from an emphasis on growth toward the direction of addressing basic human needs. In 1973, the UN Secretary-General recognized a need for the development of another indicator of progress for LDCs. Essentially, the UN desired an indicator able to tap progress in the area of human needs which remained untapped by other development indicators, such as GNP per capita (McLaughlin, 1979, p. 129). The same year, the U.S. Foreign Assistance Act of 1973 mandated that an increasing percentage of U.S. bilateral aid be directed toward the improvement of life for the poor in LDCs. The Act also mandated that new criteria be established to measure the progress within LDCs in improving the quality of life for the poor (McLaughlin, 1979, p. 129).

Measuring the quality of life in LDCs through the use of income measurements is fraught with problems that may lead to invalid and misleading figures. Productive activities in LDCs which are extraneous to the monetized economy remain unaccounted for by income measurements. Income statistics also fail to take into account the impact of government-financed services, such as free access to health care and free food distribution programs, which may alleviate some of the suffering of poverty. In response to the need for a new indicator which taps the plight of the poor, the Physical Quality of Life Index, was developed in 1977 by the Overseas Development Council under the direction of Morris D. Morris. PQLI is composed of three indicators: infant mortality, life expectancy, and adult literacy. The PQLI is a composite index which combines the three indicators, giving equal weight to each indicator (Morris, 1979).

The PQLI almost immediately gained wide acceptance internationally as a valid measure of physical well-being of the poor in LDCs (OECD, 1978). This wide acceptance is reflected by United Nations Development Program (UNDP, 1990) efforts to create a similar index. The UNDP effort is, perhaps, the only other comprehensive effort to develop a well-being indicator. The index created by the UNDP index was formulated essentially by adding per capita national income to Morris' indicators. In other words, more recent efforts to measure quality of life or well-being in LDCs have remained reasonably consistent with the PQLI developed by Morris. To date, Morris' project and the efforts of the United Nations Development Program (1990) are regarded as the most thorough measures of well-being in LDCs (Dasgupta, 1993).

Quality of life in LDCs is expected to correlate highly with GNP per capita; however, McLaughlin (1979) demonstrates through empirical study that there are a large number of exceptions to this rule and concludes that "low income and the worst consequences of absolute poverty need not go hand in hand" (McLaughlin, 1979, p. 131). Consequently, for the purposes of this research, we will employ the indicators used in the PQLI developed by Morris (1979) in order to tap quality of life in LDCs. A number of factors make the three indicators in the PQLI attractive for measuring quality of life in LDCs.

First, these indicators measure tangible results in development, directly impacting the lives of the lower classes in LDCs. For those among the lower classes in LDCs, life is often a struggle merely to survive. In such cases, deterioration of their absolute condition can only lead to malnutrition, which then will surface in aggregate figures in life expectancy rates and infant mortality rates. If the absolute conditions of the poor in LDCs do deteriorate with greater dependency and the hypothesized greater inequality, then this impact should be revealed in greater infant mortality rates, lower literacy rates, and shorter life expectancies.

PQLI not only holds allure for measuring quality of life in LDCs, but is also attractive for the purpose of this research. First, the data on life expectancy, infant mortality rates, and adult literacy are readily available for most LDCs from the World Bank over the years 1967-92 at five-year intervals. Consequently, PQLI is easily calculable from the available World Bank data on these indicators. Furthermore, PQLI has been shown to be robust as a surrogate indicator for other aspects of social progress, reflecting the combination of the effects of nutrition, public health, income, and the general environment (Morris, 1979). Simultaneously, PQLI also acts as a surrogate for other basic human needs indicators, such as access to safe water (McLaughlin, 1979). The literacy component of PQLI, according to Morris (1979), is an additional useful indicator because it reflects both well-being and a skill that is critical in the development process in LDCs. The literacy component of PQLI should tap how well the lower segments of the population are able to share in the benefits of economic growth, as well as reflect the status of women in society (Morris, 1979). PQLI has also been shown to be nonethnocentric, non-susceptible to exchange rates, and objective in character (Morris, 1979). A final advantage of PQLI is that it may provide insight into the impact of regime type on the plight of the poor in LDCs (McLaughlin, 1979). Consequently, the independent variables for dependency will be regressed on PQLI in order to determine whether dependency is associated with quality of life in LDCs.

Quality Improvement

PQLI, however, as a dependent variable is not without its shortcomings. The usage of PQLI as a dependent variable may lack explanatory power regarding the question of whether dependency perpetuates a lower physical quality of life in LDCs. It is possible that the indicators of dependency will be negatively associated with PQLI, yet not be associated with factors which perpetuate lower PQLI. In other words, the possibility may remain that dependency is merely a characteristic of states which suffer from lower levels of PQLI and not a factor which causes or perpetuates lower levels of PQLI. In order to determine whether this is indeed the case, the relationship between dependency and PQLI growth (Quality Improvement) must be investigated.

Even if dependency does prove to be negatively related to PQLI, we argue that a positive relationship (or no relationship) between dependency and Quality

Improvement would undermine the argument that dependency perpetuates lower PQLI. Instead, such results would suggest that dependency does not perpetuate low PQLI. Quality Improvement will be measured as the percentage change in PQLI over each five-year period under analysis. The data analyzed representing the indicators of dependency are from the years 1972, 1977, 1982, 1987, and 1992. The data analyzed representing Quality Improvement are taken from the years 1967-72, 1973-77, 1978-82, 1983-87, and 1988-92.

Control Variables

In the following section, the independent variables which are chosen to be included in the analysis as control variables are introduced and the rationale behind their selection is discussed. Included in the discussion of each variable is a discussion of its use in previous empirical studies.

Regime Type

Clearly, a multitude of variables, both internal and external, affect growth, inequality, and quality of life in LDCs. Failure to control for factors that may confound the relationship between dependency and the dependent variables is a weakness in much of the literature analyzing the effects of dependency.

Scholars have long debated the relationship between democracy and development. Lipset (1959) observed a statistically significant positive relationship between democracy and growth. Conversely, Milton Friedman (1981) argues that while capitalism is a necessary, but not sufficient, condition for the development of democracy, democracy hinders growth through the creation of a noncompetitive welfare state. Friedman argues that democratic governments have ventured into activities which should instead be performed by the private sector including price supports, tariffs, nontariff barriers, interest and wage rates, social safety nets, and the regulation of industry. In the end, Friedman contends that the tendency of modern democracy to collectivize hinders productivity. It must be noted, however that Friedman (1982, p. 59) also makes the apparently contradictory argument that political freedom is a necessary condition for economic freedom. Since Friedman argues that the free and unfettered market is the most efficient avenue to economic growth and political freedom is necessary for a free market, then Friedman is also inferring that authoritarian regimes hinder growth because they hinder the free market. What can be perhaps concluded from Friedman's contradictory arguments then is that it is not regime type at all with which he is concerned, but the free market.

Concurring with Friedman's (1981) arguments is the work of William Mitchell (1988). Mitchell argues that failures of political performance are inherent properties of the political process. According to Mitchell (1988, p. 109), "inequity, inefficiency, and coercion are the most general results of democratic policy formation." Mitchell contends that the public demand for services in a democracy turns society into a "special interest," "rent seeking" society. Similarly, Mancur Olson (1982) argues that the behavior of individuals and firms in stable democracies leads to the formation of powerful interest groups whose demands on government render economies less efficient.

These liberal scholars are not alone in their view that regime types may be important determinants of economic development. Dependency scholars, Cardoso and Faletto (1979), infer that authoritarian regimes are necessary for associated dependent development in LDCs due to the disturbances which are created by inequality and other problems associated with that type of development. Similarly, Guillermo O'Donnell (1973) links dependency with regime type in his argument that dependency produces bureaucratic-authoritarian states. Essentially, the argument is that dependent growth produces inequality which leads to authoritarianism in order to quell the civil unrest which may be produced through the inequality. Hence, the inference is that growth in dependent economies is only possible under authoritarian regimes and due to inequalities produced by dependent growth. Clearly a significant group of dependency scholars are of the opinion that regime type has a significant relationship with both growth and inequality. Most important for the purposes of this research is the contention of Cardoso and Faletto that authoritarian regimes are necessary for associated dependent development. The expectations of these dependency theorists would be for growth to be more rapid in LDCs with authoritarian regimes than with democratic regimes (the authoritarian regime being necessary to suppress discontent of the masses due to rising inequality produced from dependency). Hence, Cardoso and Faletto are also inferring that authoritarian regimes allow greater income inequality.

A major inference of the associated-dependent development thesis is that the lower classes suffer a deterioration of their physical quality of life due to dependency induced inequality and authoritarianism. Empirical studies linking regime type to physical quality of life have produced evidence which is unsupportive of this thesis. Edgar Owens (1987) argues that some governments which he labels as "populist authoritarian" tend to be positively associated with physical quality of life. Frank W. Young (1990) tests Owens' hypothesis and concludes that there is a positive association between "populist authoritarian" regimes and physical quality of life. Though these studies support the notion that regime type is important for explaining physical quality of life, it must be noted that physical quality of life is measured through the use of a single indicator (life expectancy) and the data gathered were representative of only one year. Furthermore, the criteria for the classification of regimes as "populist authoritarian" is admittedly somewhat subjective and includes Cuba and the People's Republic of China, yet omits states which would be seemingly populist authoritarian such as Chile (Young, 1990, p. 352).

Despite these deficiencies, the studies do provide empirical support for the inclusion of regime as a control variable when investigating the relationship between dependency and physical quality of life. It must be noted, however, that all scholars do not view regime types as important determinants of economic development. Karen Remmer (1990) in a study of the Latin American debt crisis in 1982 concludes that regime type is a generally unimportant variable for explaining the ability of LDCs to handle economic crises. Instead, Remmer cites ideology, the structure of decision-making, and the composition of governing coalitions as more important for handling economic crises than regime type.

For the purposes of this research, regime type must be included as a control variable when investigating the relationships between dependency and growth, inequality, and PQLI due to its emphasis by dependency scholars. Data on regime type will be gathered from the Freedom House publication by Raymond Gastil for the years 1977, 1982, 1987, and 1992. Data for 1972 will be gathered from Freedom House (1973). The regime data for 1967 will be gathered and coded from Arthur S. Banks' Cross-Sectional Time Series Data (1971). Regime type will be coded as a dummy variable with a one entered for democracies and a zero for nondemocratic states.

Freedom House codes the regimes on a three point ordinal scale ranging from not free, to somewhat free, and free. Careful investigation of the Gastil/Freedom House coding reveals that the states which are labeled as "somewhat free" should be lumped together with states coded as "not free" since these states yet lack many of the elements necessary to be considered something other than authoritarian. For example, Bahrain in 1982 is coded as partly free by Gastil and Freedom House despite the fact that it was a "traditional shaikhdom" and the legislature had been dissolved (Gastil, 1984, p. 332). Similarly, Bangladesh in 1982 was coded as partly free despite the reintroduction of military rule in 1982 (Gastil, 1984, p. 333). Consequently, for the purposes of this research, the states coded by Gastil/Freedom House as partly free will be recoded as not free in a dichotomous variable.

GNP Per Capita as Control

Several studies suggest that the effects of dependency are confounded by the wealth of LDCs. Bornschier et al. (1978) and Dolan and Tomlin (1980) argue that the effects of dependency are greater in LDCs with greater wealth. Similarly, Bornschier et al. (1978) argue that foreign investment and aid tend to go to states with relatively higher levels of economic development because wealthier states offer greater investment opportunities. Therefore, level of wealth may be expected to correlate with direct foreign investment and confound the dependency relationship. On the other hand, Gobalet and Diamond (1979) argue that the effects of dependency are more acute in LDCs which are poorer.

In regard to the dependent variable PQLI, GNP per capita has been shown to be the best predictor of physical quality of life in a study by Stewart (1985, p. 58). Similarly, Mosk and Johansson (1986) conclude that there is a causal link between GNP per capita and efficient health technology and mortality rates. Consequently, the inclusion of GNP per capita as a control variable when investigating PQLI is a necessity.

Intuitively, we expect wealth to have an effect on the dependency-growth-equity relationship since wealthier countries (with the exception of oil states) are perhaps less likely to exhibit monocultural economies. We also would expect a greater possibility for very large increases or decreases in GNP per capita growth among the states with very low GNP per capita. Consequently, level of wealth as measured by GNP per capita will be introduced into the analysis as a control variable when investigating the dependency relationship for GNP per capita growth, inequality, PQLI, and PQLI growth.

Gross National Product

Bornschier et al. (1980) argue that the previously mentioned observed relationship between wealth and dependency is a spurious relationship. Instead, Bornschier et al. argue that the interaction is with the size of the economy itself. The conclusions of Bornschier et al. are that since wealth and market size are correlated among LDCs, a spuriously stronger effect is observed if size is not controlled for. Similarly, Jackson (1979) argues that in measuring the level of integration between the periphery and the core, one must control for the size of the peripheral economy. Jackson's basic argument is that figures for core penetration only have explanatory power if weighted by their importance to the periphery production. Intuitively, we expect that market size may have a great impact on the relationships between dependency and all of the dependent variables since larger economies are perhaps less likely to exhibit monoculture in production or severe concentration of trading partners. Consequently, for the purposes of this research, the size of the economy as indicated by GNP will be introduced into the analysis as a control variable when investigating the relationships between dependency and each of the dependent variables.

Population Growth

Bornschier and Ballmer-Cao (1978) argue that the effects of dependence on economic growth are mediated by population growth. Their hypothesis is that population growth is inversely related to growth in GNP per capita since economies are unable to grow fast enough to account for rapid population growth. Consequently, observed negative relationships between dependency and GNP growth may be spurious if controls for population growth are not implemented. Similarly, population growth must be controlled for when investigating the relationship between dependency and quality of life since population growth, that exceeds GNP growth, is widely viewed as increasing marginalization (Birdsall, 1984). Essentially, an expanding population increases the rate of consumption. In a world of finite resources, this necessarily reduces savings and capital accumulation. In such cases, the population growth essentially outstrips the ability of the economy to provide employment and basic services; consequently, quality of life diminishes. Hence, population growth will be used as a control variable when investigating the dependency relationships.

Area

Although no previous studies (that we are aware of) have controlled for area, it is perhaps a great error that they have not. We argue that many of the problems of LDCs such as monocultural economies and trade partner concentration may be very much related to area. It appears to be only common sense that area is highly correlated with natural resource endowment and diversity in agricultural production. Unless area is controlled for, it cannot be shown that slow growth and inequality are more the byproducts of external factors than merely the byproducts of having insufficient area for states to be self sufficient. Furthermore, large geographic area in LDCs may be a hindrance to building the necessary infrastructure (roads, railways, proper sanitation facilities) which can lead to improvements in physical quality of life. Hence, LDCs with large geographic area may have to spend a greater percentage of their resources on infrastructure in order to achieve the same gains in physical quality of life as other LDCs. Consequently, total area in square miles will be utilized as a control variable when investigating the relationship between dependency and each of the dependent variables.

GNP Per Capita Growth as Control

In analysis of the relationship between dependency and inequality, PQLI, and PQLI growth, per capita GNP growth must be controlled for since it has been hypothesized (Huntington and Nelson, 1976) that growth and inequality may be related. Furthermore, in an empirical study Kaufman et al. (1975) find that income inequality is positively related to dependency, but also positively related to growth. Consequently, when growth is controlled for, Kaufman et al. conclude that it is growth which produces the inequality, not dependency. States with higher growth rates may experience greater degrees of inequality; consequently, failure to control for growth could confound the dependency-equity relationship. Similarly, growth must be controlled for when investigating the dependency-PQLI relationship since decreases in PQLI could easily result from negative growth rather than from dependency. Furthermore, Pourgerami (1991) links growth to democracy, freedom, and human rights which are expected by both the liberal and dependency paradigms to increase physical quality of life in LDCs.

Inequality as Control

Since the basic argument of Cardoso and Faletto (1979) is that dependency has a deleterious effect on the lower classes through inequality, inequality will be utilized as a control variable when investigating the relationships between dependency and the dependent variables, PQLI and Quality Improvement. Essentially, Cardoso and Faletto infer that PQLI will be lower under conditions of greater inequality. Whether or not this assumption is correct is dependent on the type of inequality which exists. If inequality is due to a deteriorating condition of the lower classes, then Cardoso and Faletto may be correct in their inference that inequality has deleterious effects on PQLI. Conversely, if the main cause of inequality is a rising income for the upper classes while the income of the lower classes remains constant or increases at a slower rate, then inequality would be of little utility in explaining PQLI. We expect that dependency theorists are correct in their assertion that the upper classes are the classes which benefit the most in dependent economies, however, as the upper classes benefit (producing greater inequality) this does not in and of itself have a negative effect on PQLI. Consequently, we expect inequality to be unrelated to PQLI and Quality Improvement.

PQLI as Control

When investigating the relationship between dependency and PQLI growth, PQLI must be included as a control variable, for the same reasons that GNP must be controlled for when investigating GNP per capita growth. Essentially, the potential for rapid growth in PQLI is greater among states with very low PQLIs. Access to safe water or modern medical supplies may produce rapid growth in PQLI among states that previously did not enjoy such benefits, but tend to diminish in their return in terms of PQLI growth as states increase their physical quality of life. Furthermore, since PQLI is essentially a finite relational scale from zero to one hundred, the mathematical possibility of high percentage growth in PQLI diminishes the nearer states get to one hundred. For example, it is possible for a state with a PQLI of 50 to grow 100 percent in PQLI (in other words, essentially double) to a score of 100. Conversely, a state with a higher PQLI of say 75 cannot increase its PQLI score more than 33 percent (a total of 25 points) because the highest possibility on the relational scale is 100. Hence, PQLI will be utilized as a control in the analysis of the relationship between dependency and PQLI growth.

Data

We propose to determine the relationships between dependency and each of the dependent variables, GNP per capita, GNP per capita growth, inequality, PQLI, and PQLI growth, through the employment of pooled cross-sectional time-series analysis. The advantage of combining cross-sectional data and time series in this manner, according to Sayrs (1989, p. 2), is to "capture variation across different units in space, as well as variation that emerges over time. We are thus able to describe, analyze, and test hypotheses about outcomes and the processes that generate the outcomes." In other words, the pooled cross-sectional time-series design allows the testing of the hypotheses over space and time simultaneously, therefore, allowing the observation of phenomena which are unobservable in cross-sectional analysis. Time series analysis allows the advantage of both explaining the past and predicting the future behavior of related phenomena (Ostrom, 1991, p. 5).

The data will be pooled from samples taken at five year intervals beginning in 1967 and ending in 1992. These years were selected due to the limited data availability from the World Bank on the quality of life indicators (which are only available in five year intervals). This data set does include the more recent time period which has yet to be subjected to rigorous analysis. The dependent variables, growth, inequality, and quality of life, will all be analyzed separately with the independent and control variables.

The countries under analysis are those not considered to by high income by the World Bank as of 1992. Countries for which data are missing in quantities sufficient to confound the analysis are omitted from the analysis. Consequently, all of the former communist bloc states as well as some other states for which the World Bank has been unable to gather sufficient data are omitted since these countries did not belong to the World Bank.

When separate Generalized Least Squares Autoregressive Moving Average (GLS-ARMA) operations are performed on each of the dependent variables for the indicators of dependency observed for all LDCs, the possible diverse patterns of dependency should emerge. The data over the 26-year time period should be long enough to draw conclusions regarding the long term effects of dependency on the dependent variables. Due to the emphasis of earlier research on the periods of the 1950's and 1960's, the analysis of the 1967-1992 time period is not only a venture into uncharted waters, but it avoids redundancy.

The pooled cross-sectional time series design is susceptible to several endogenous problems for which we must test and correct. Specifically, we acknowledge that problems of multicolinearity, autocorrelation, and heteroskedasticity must be addressed. These potential problems are discussed below.

Multicolinearity, Heteroskedasticity, and Autoregression

If multicolinearity does indeed prove to present itself as a problem in the independent variables selected for this research, then we intend to correct for the multicolinearity through a combination of the independent variables through factor analysis. Berry and Feldman (1989, p. 48) argue that variables should only be combined when they are multiple indicators of the same theoretical concept. For complete discussions of the effects of multicolinearity, see Fox (1991) and Berry and Feldman (1989).

Heteroskedasticity does not present a problem for the Generalized Least Squares Autoregressive Moving Average (GLS-ARMA) procedure which will be employed in this analysis since the normal specification for the GLS-ARMA model is heteroskedastic error. In other words, the estimator includes a weighted least squares analog where the weight is the inverse of ordinary least squares residual variance by cross-section. Micro-Crunch software allows users to override that default by specifying that variances on each cross-section must be equalized. In other words, the GLS-ARMA model included in Micro-Crunch allows users to force homoskedasticity. For a more in-depth discussion of this procedure see Stimson (1985).

Autocorrelation will be detected through the use of the Durbin-Watson statistic which is calculated through the use of the GLS-ARMA technique in Micro-Crunch. GLS ARMA is a generalized least squares specification which incorporates an autoregressive moving average specification for error in the time-serial dimension. A Durbin-Watson statistic must be produced in a range between -1 and 2 for the statistics produced through the GLS-ARMA technique to be reliable. If the Durbin-Watson statistic falls outside of this range, dummy variables will be added for each case where variance ratios are in excess of 1.0 in hopes that the problem can be eradicated. A more complete discussion of this procedure is offered by Stimson (1985).

Overview of Operations

The following five tables (Tables 4.1, 4.2, 4.3, 4.4, and 4.5) represent the basic equations, as discussed above, which will be utilized for investigation of the relationship between dependency, growth, equity, and quality of life.

Table 4.1: Operationalization: Dependency and GNP per capita

Independent Variables	Control Variables	Dependent Variable
Core Trade Volume % GNP	GNP	
% Trade with largest 2 Core states	Population Growth	
Debt % GNP	Area	
Aid % GNP	GNP Per Ca. Growth	
Foreign Investment % GNP	Regime Type	GNP per Capita
Foreign Patent Registrations		
Energy Imports as % Consumption		
Nonfuel primary % of exports		

Table 4.2: Operationalization: Dependency and Growth

Independent Variables	Control Variables	Dependent Variable
Core Trade Volume % GNP	GNP	
% Trade with largest 2 Core states	Population Growth	
Debt % GNP	Area	
Aid % GNP	GNP per capita	
Foreign Investment % GNP	Regime Type	GNP per cap growth
domestic patent registrations		
Energy Imports as % Consumption		
Nonfuel primary % of exports		

Table 4.3: Operationalization: Dependency and Inequality

Independent Variables	Control Variables	Dependent Variable
Core Trade Volume % GNP	GNP	
% Trade with largest 2 Core states	Population Growth	
Debt % GNP	Area	
Aid % GNP	GNP per Cap Growth	
Foreign Investment % GNP	GNP per Capita	Inequality
Patent Registrations	Regime Type	
Energy Imports as % Consumption		
Nonfuel primary % of exports		

Table 4.4: Operationalization: Dependency and PQLI

Independent Variables	Control Variables	Dependent Variable
Core Trade Volume % GNP	GNP	
% Trade with largest 2 Core states	Population Growth	
Debt % GNP	Area	
Aid % GNP	GNP per Cap Growth	
Foreign Investment % GNP	GNP per Capita	PQLI
Patent Registrations	Regime Type	
Energy Imports as % Consumption		
Nonfuel primary % of exports		

Table 4.5: Operationalization: Dependency and Quality Improvement

Independent Variables	Control Variables	Dependent Variable
Core Trade Volume % GNP	Population Growth	
% Trade with largest 2 Core states	Area	
Debt % GNP	GNP per Capita	
Aid % GNP	GNP per Cap Growth	
Foreign Investment % GNP	Regime Type	PQLI Growth
Foreign Patent Registrations	PQLI	
Energy Imports/ Energy Cnsmptn.	GNP	
Nonfuel primary as % exports		

The results should not only provide the researcher with information about how important dependency is in explaining the variance in growth, inequality, and physical quality of life in LDCs, but also provide important insight into which aspects of dependency are most important among the dependency indicators, including clientelism. If the variables prove to explain a large percentage of the variance in growth, inequality, and PQLI, then dependency theory may be supported—especially if the observed relationships prove to be negative. If, however, the variables included are unable to explain a majority of the variance, the dependency perspective will be unsupported. Failure to explain a large percentage of the variance is suggestive that internal factors may be more important in explaining growth, inequality, and PQLI than external factors of dependency.

The importance of this research is multiple in character. First, this research design fills a void in the literature by providing comprehensive analysis of the dependency-growth-equity relationship rather than merely a focus on one or a few limited aspects of dependency such as direct foreign investment. Secondly, the empirical analysis utilizes a pooled time series design which, has not been extensively employed. Thirdly, this research apparently is the first effort which addresses the question of the impact of dependency on the quality of life in LDCs, rather than merely the condition of the poor in a relative sense. Additionally, more control variables are included than in any previous research we have reviewed, including area, which has inexplicably been omitted by all previous scholars. From both a theoretical and a methodological point of view, the inclusion of growth as a control variable is apparently a pioneering effort in empirical analysis of dependency relationships and should be invaluable in investigating the possibly spurious relationship between dependency and inequality. Similarly, the inclusion of regime type in the analysis of dependency is noteworthy since scholars have not addressed the possible impacts of this variable in the analysis of dependency and physical quality of life. In short, this research should provide valuable information which may either support, or disparage, the dependency positions which hold that dependency produces "underdevelopment," inequality, and adverse effects on the physical quality of life in LDCs.

Finally, this research has clear relevance to the world of politics and policy formation outside of scholarly research. In other words, the findings of this research should have clear policy implications contingent on its results. If results are conclusive that dependency tends to foster growth, does not foster gross inequalities, and is not detrimental to quality of life in LDCs, then the present course of marketization and integration for both core and periphery appears reasonable if economic development is the goal. However, if results significantly support dependency theory, then both core and periphery should perhaps reexamine their current policy course and consider shifting away from marketization, integration, and dependent relationships, if growth, some degree of equity, and some kind of betterment of the quality of life are desired goals.

Without empirical analysis which subjects dependency theory to rigorous tests, the discussions between modernization and dependency advocates may be little more than exercises in comparative propaganda. Furthermore, it is perhaps even a greater travesty when an idea such as dependency theory could continue to receive so much attention if it is for the most part unsupported by empirical evidence. Obviously, the economic successes of Taiwan, South Korea, Hong Kong, and Singapore present dependency theory with some serious problems, since it appears that all of these states would test to be heavily dependent, yet have attained rapid rates of sustained growth and reasonable equity. Dependency theorists generally argue that such "isolated" cases are outliers (O'Hearn, 1989); in other words, these four Asian success stories are viewed by dependency theorists as exceptions to the norm. Through the research project developed in this paper, it may empirically be determined whether the Asian cases are indeed outliers or deviant cases as dependency advocates argue, or are instead, in fact, the norm.

Chapter 5

Factor and Bivariate Analyses

Introduced below is the sample which will be utilized for the analysis of the relationships between dependency and dependent variables. After the introduction of the sample, the interrelationships among the independent dependency indicators will be explored through factor analysis. The factor analysis should reveal whether the eight independent variables selected as indicators of dependency operate independently of one another or whether it is possible to derive a smaller number of distinct patterns or dimensions from the eight independent variables.

Along with factor analysis, bivariate relationships between all of the independent and dependent variables will also be investigated to examine both the direction and strength. The analysis may also be useful for understanding the utility of the control variables. Dependency theory would expect strong positive associations between the dependent variables and energy independence and technological independence and negative associations between the dependent variables and all other dependency indicators. Conversely, dependency theorists would expect little relationship between the control variables and the dependent variables since the control variables are representative of internal rather than external factors and dependency theory holds that economic development is largely determined by external factors (Chilcote and Edelstein, 1974).

The Sample

The sample of countries includes LDCs which are classified as low or middle-income states by the World Bank: 36 African countries, 22 Latin American countries, 14 Asian countries, 3 European (including Turkey) and 1 Oceanic state (Papua New Guinea). Of the African countries, 29 are from sub-Saharan Africa (including South Africa) and 7 from the North African Saharan region. Asian countries include, 4 from the Middle East (5 if one includes Turkey), 5 South Asian, 2 East Asian, and 3 from Southeast Asia. Most of the Middle Eastern states are not included in the sample because they are now in the high-income category according to the World Bank. The former Communist Bloc states are omitted from the sample due to insufficient data.

The time period covers 26 years at five year intervals beginning in 1967 and ending in 1992. These years were chosen due to data availability from the World Bank particularly on life expectancy and infant mortality which are measures of PQLI. Although it is unfortunate that all LDCs are not included due to insufficient data, the sample includes a broad cross-section and should be sufficient to provide f: a valid cross-national test of dependency and assess the impact of dependency on economic development.

Dependency: One-Dimensional or Multidimensional?

The next step in our analysis is to investigate the interrelationships among the independent variables through factor analysis. According to Mahler (1980, p. 42) "the most powerful statistical tool for exploring relationships among a large number of variables is factor analysis." Factor analysis is a technique which allows the extraction of a smaller set of factors that are composites of related variables weighted according to their contribution from a larger set of variables. If a smaller number of composite variables explains a substantial proportion of the variance in the original variables, then a clearer picture of a simpler structure inherent in the original variables is produced. If, however, no such simpler structure exists, any factors that emerge will be weak and indiscriminate, and in that case less enlightening than the original variables (Mahler, 1980, p. 42).

As previously discussed, dependency theorists (Duvall, 1978; Caporaso, 1980) tend to view dependency as a holistic concept of elements which cannot be analyzed separately. On the basis of this holistic idea, one would expect all of the indicators of dependency to be part of the same conceptual dimension. Conversely, dependency is often referred to by scholars as a multidimensional and complex concept (Jackson, 1979; Packenham, 1986). Empirical studies to date have tended to treat dependency as such a multidimensional concept (Bornschier et al., 1978). Hence, in discussing the effects of dependency such as unequal exchange, bureaucratic authoritarianism, and income inequality, dependency theorists tend to treat the concept of dependency both as monolithic and as multidimensional. Examples of this type of treatment of dependency are legion, but for our purposes we refer to the previous review of dependency literature. On the basis of the empirical analysis of previous scholars, we do not expect dependency to emerge as a unidimensional concept.

In previous empirical studies, dependency has emerged as a multidimensional concept through the employment of factor analysis. Schmitter (1971) and West (1973) found that a number of different dimensions of external dependency emerged. Similarly, Kaufman et al. (1975) collected data on four indicators of "trade" dependence and four indicators of "capital" dependence with the expectation that two dimensions would be extracted. From the factor analysis, however, three distinct factor loadings emerged, and one indicator did not load highly on any factor. Consequently, Kaufman et al. did not make use of the factors for any further analysis.

Table 5.1 contains the results of the factor analysis performed on the eight dependency indicators. A varimax rotation of the factors is utilized in order to clarify the patterns and to maximize the differences which might be present. Similar to the findings of Kaufman et al. (1975), three factors emerge from the analysis. In the rotated factor matrix, trade as a percentage of GNP (core trade), debt as a percentage of GNP (debt dependency), aid as a percentage of GNP (aid), and patents (technological independence) all load on factor one. Energy production as a percentage of consumption (energy independence) and reliance on nonfuel primary products in exports (primary exports) load on the second factor and direct foreign investment (dfi) as a percentage of GNP and trade partner concentration (trade concentration) load on the third factor. It must be noted, however, that core trade and aid dependency each substantially load on two factors, suggesting that the patterns are not completely distinct from one another.

Table 5.1: Rotated Factor Matrix

Variable	Factor 1	Factor 2	Factor 3
Trade % GNP	**.62813**	.42332	-.24820
Trade Concentration.	.09988	.08521	**-.75575**
Debt %GNP	**.68268**	-.14083	.25727
Aid %GNP	**.57010**	-.46040	.19407
DFI%GNP	.11767	.19954	**.63496**
Energy Prod%Con	.04421	**.69122**	.07677
Primary Exports	.28860	**-.75409**	-.08521
Patents	**-.58853**	.08346	.11358

The utility of the factors for analysis of external dependence is questionable for several reasons. First, the loadings of patents with core trade, debt, and aid create labeling problems. Precisely what concept or dimension is represented by each factor is unclear and labeling would entail what is, perhaps, excessive subjectivity on the part of the researcher. Secondly, the loading of the variables on three factors is inconsistent with the holistic concept of dependency. Finally, the labeling problem associated with the factors creates major problems of interpretation of statistical results in multivariate analysis. The valid interpretation of the B coefficients produced in multivariate analysis is seriously compromised when one is unable to sensibly and precisely label or define the factor itself. In this sense, the B coefficients involving the dependency indicators individually will lend greater validity to conclusions based on the results. Consequently, we intend to follow the lead of West (1973), and Kaufman et al. (1975) and abandon the usage of the factors which have emerged from the analysis in favor of utilization of the dependency indicators separately in the multivariate analysis.

Bivariate Analysis

In this section, bivariate analysis of the independent variables are presented. The Pearson product moment correlations are computed and presented for all of the variables involved in the analysis. The underlying purpose for which the bivariate relationships are analyzed is to provide a picture of association between the variables. The bivariate analysis should be useful in supporting or failing to support the arguments of dependency theorists that there is an association between dependency and underdevelopment.

Dependency theorists would expect the dependency indicators to exhibit strong bivariate relationships with the dependent variables. Energy independence and technological independence should exhibit strong positive relationships and all of the other dependency indicators should exhibit strong negative relationships with the dependent variables in order to be consistent with dependency expectations. Similarly, dependency theorists (Chilcote and Edelstein, 1974; Jackson, 1979) infer that the elements which compose dependency are working in concert to produce deleterious economic effects. Thus, in order to be consistent with dependency expectations, energy independence and technological independence should be positively associated, but negatively associated with the other dependency indicators. The remaining six dependency indicators should be positively associated with each other, but negatively associated with energy and technological independence. Importantly, dependency theorists would not expect the control variables to be strongly associated with the dependent variables since the control variables represent internal elements which are unaccounted for by dependency theory (Chilcote and Edelstein, 1974). In short, the observed Pearson product moment correlations should be useful in gaining insight into the nature of the associations between all of the variables and provide a basis for the claims of dependency theory. The results will reveal whether the dependency relationships (if they do indeed exist at all) are readily observable, or if they are perhaps obscured by other factors which confound the associations.

First, the results of bivariate analysis involving only the independent dependency variables will be presented. Presentation of the results of bivariate analysis involving the dependency and control variables follows, and finally, the results of the bivariate analysis involving dependency, control, and dependent variables are presented.

Bivariate Relationships: Independent Variables

Table 5.2 presented below reports the correlation matrix for the eight independent variables selected for measuring dependency. A number of noteworthy relationships emerge which merit discussion. First, the signs which emerge are in many cases inconsistent with the expectations of dependency theory. Energy independence is positively associated with trade concentration in a statistically significant correlation. Similarly, trade concentration exhibited a statistically significant negative correlation with aid contrary to the expectations of dependency theory. In general, however, the variables prove to be statistically significant in the direction predicted by dependency theory in nine of the eleven cases. The results are far from conclusive since statistical significance is achieved in only eleven of the twenty-eight relationships; however, nine of the eleven statistically significant correlations conform to the direction which is consistent with dependency theory.

More support for this statement is found in the relative weakness of the correlations. The strongest statistically significant relationships are observed between aid and debt (correlation .36) and between aid and primary exports (correlation .37). No other correlations were observed to exceed .25. Furthermore, no statistically significant relationships were observed involving direct foreign investment. The relatively low correlations between all of the independent variables suggest similar conclusions regarding all of the dependency variables. In other words, the dependency indicators appear to be largely unrelated and operating independently of one another. In general, the results of the bivariate analysis on the independent variables, similar to the factor results, suggest that dependency is conceptually complex and multidimensional rather than monolithic in character and may be in some instances multidirectional in character.

Table 5.2: Correlation Matrix: Independent Variables

	e	f	g	h	i	j	o
d	*.16	*.17	*.05	-.09	.14	-.14	*-.14
e		-.08	*-.08	-.08	*05	-.0	-.06
f			*.36	.11	-.09	*.15	-.13
g				.01	-.10	*.37	*-.22
h					-.01	-.10	-.02
i						-.25	-.03
j							*-.23

Key
* Statistically significant at .05 level.
Positive Correlations in Bold
Negative correlations in italics.

d= trade with core as a percentage of GNP (core trade)
e=trade with top two core trade partners as a percentage of total trade (trade concentration)
f= external debt as a percentage of GNP (debt)
g= aid receipts as a percentage of GNP (aid)
h= direct foreign investment as a percentage of GNP (dfi)
i= energy production as a percentage of energy consumption (energy independence)
j= exports of nonfuel primary products as a percentage of total exports (primary exports)
o= patents granted (technological independence)

Bivariate Relationships: Dependency and Control Variables

Below, in Table 5.3, is a correlation matrix relating all of the dependency and control variables. The expectations regarding the bivariate relationships between dependency and the control variables are not altogether clear from the dependency perspective in a directional sense.

Table 5.3: Correlations: Dependency and Control Variables

	e	f	g	h	i	j	l	m	n	o	Ad
d	***16**	***17**	***05**	*09*	**14**	*14*	**14*	**09**	***21**	**14*	**05**
e		*08*	***08**	**08**	***05**	*0*	*05*	**05**	*10*	*06*	***09**
f			***36**	**11**	*09*	***15**	*10*	**06**	*08*	*13*	**02**
g				**01**	*10*	***37**	*25*	**12**	*17*	**22*	***10**
h					*01*	*10*	**02**	*02*	**01**	*02*	**04**
i						*25*	**02**	**12**	**01**	*03*	**0**
j							**38*	**04**	*11*	**23*	***13**
l								*09*	***61**	***55**	**09**
m									**05**	*14*	**07**
n										***42**	**04**
o											**01**

Key
* Statistically significant at .05 level
Negative correlations in italics
Positive correlations in bold

d= core trade as a percentage of GNP
e= trade partner concentration
f= external debt as % GNP
g= aid receipts as a percentage of GNP
h= dir. For. Investment as % of GNP
i= energy prod. as % consumption

j= nonfuel primary products as % exports
l= GNP
m= population growth
n= area in square miles
o= patents granted
ad= regime

Dependency theorists tend not to address the relationship between dependency and factors which could confound the relationship between dependency and development. The lone exception to this is the regime variable which dependency theorists (O'Donnell, 1973; Cardoso, 1973) expect to be negatively associated with dependency. O'Donnell (1973) and Cardoso (1973) argue that dependency leads to populist pressures within LDCs that require the installation of authoritarian states in order to control them. Unlike O'Donnell and Cardoso, we do not expect a negative association between dependency and democratic regimes. Furthermore, unlike dependency theorists, we expect the control variables to exhibit associations with dependency which tend to obscure the relationships between dependency and the dependent variables.

The relationships between the dependency indicators and the control variables prove to be mixed or multidirectional in character. The control variable which perhaps best exemplifies this multidirectional character is the regime variable. Contrary to the tenets of dependency theory, democratic regimes are revealed to have statistically significant positive associations with trade partner concentration. Conversely, democratic regimes proved to exhibit statistically significant negative associations with aid and reliance on raw material exports, as dependency theorists would suggest. Consequently, the associations regarding the regime variable are, in some cases, consistent and others inconsistent with dependency expectations.

In contrast to the significant results that were observed regarding regime and area, there were no relationships involving population growth which proved to be statistically significant; however, it remains possible that population growth may exhibit significant associations with the dependency variables when all other variables are held constant in multivariate analysis.

In general the control variables produced Pearson product moment correlations which are greater than those involving the dependency variables only. The correlations between GNP and area (.61), GNP and technological independence (.55), GNP and primary exports (-.38), and area and technological independence (.42) are larger than any of the relationships that did not include the control variables. Area also exhibits an important (-.21) association with core trade. These strong relationships suggest that area and GNP may be important factors which could confound the relationships between dependency and the dependent variables.

The results suggest that reliance on primary exports may be a factor associated with smaller economies rather than by contact between LDCs and core states. Technological independence also appears to be associated with the size of the economy as represented by GNP. The .55 positive correlation between technological independence and GNP is difficult to explain through dependency theory since the internal factor of economic size is strongly associated with technological independence. Similarly, area and technological independence produced a strong positive (.42) correlation, suggesting that technological independence is also explained by the geographic size of the country rather than through contact between core states and LDCs. Finally, the very strong (.61) positive correlation between the control variable area and GNP reveals that states with relatively small area in square miles tend to also have relatively small economic production. Other than these five relationships, however, the results of the bivariate analysis produce weak associations, in general, with no other statistically significant correlations exceeding .14. In this respect, the control variables are perhaps more conspicuous for their lack of relationships with the dependency variables, than for their association.

Bivariate Relationships: Control and Dependent Variables

Table 5.4 presents the correlation matrix for all of the independent, control, and dependent variables. The relationships involving each dependent variable will be discussed individually followed by a summary of the bivariate analysis.

Table 5.4: Composite Correlation Matrix

	e	f	g	h	i	j	k	l	m	n	o	p	q	u	y	Ad
d	***16**	***17**	***05**	**09**	*14*	*14*	**23**	**14*	**09**	**21*	**14*	**18**	**47**	**22**	*09*	**05**
e		*08*	***08**	*08*	**05**	**0*	**01*	*05*	**05**	*10*	*06*	*02*	**09**	***12**	**13*	***09**
f			***36**	**11**	*09*	**15*	*10*	*10*	**06**	*08*	*13*	*19*	**06**	*02*	*02*	**02**
g				**01**	*10*	***37**	***29**	***25**	**12**	*17*	**22*	*12*	*01*	***46**	***26**	***10**
h					*01*	*10*	**02**	**02**	*02*	*01*	*02*	**0**	*08*	*0*	*03*	*04*
i						*25*	**04**	*02*	**12**	*01*	*03*	**06**	*04*	*02*	**17*	**0**
j							***52**	**38*	**04**	*11*	**23*	**22*	***25**	**35*	**15**	**13*
k								***39**	**05**	*13*	**18*	**27*	**10**	***43**	***19**	***34**
l									*09*	**61*	**55*	**15**	**04**	**25**	*13*	**09**
m										*05*	*14*	*02*	**16**	**30**	**17**	**07**
n											**42*	*03*	**23**	**01**	*03*	**04**
o												**08**	**07**	**25**	*14*	**01**
p													*07*	**09**	*07*	**07**
q														**10**	*0*	*02*
u															**45*	***39**
y																**18*

*Statistically significant at .05 level   *Negative correlations in italics*   **Positive correlations in bold**

d= core trade	i= energy independence	n= area
e= trade concentration	j= primary exports	o=tech. independence
f.= debt as % GNP	k= GNP per capita	p=GNP per capita growth
g= aid as % GNP	l= GNP	q=inequality
h=dir. foreign investment	m=pop.growth	ad=regime

Dependency and GNP per Capita

Dependency theorists would expect negative relationships between dependency and GNP per capita since dependency is theorized to contribute to "underdevelopment." Hence, GNP per capita should be positively associated with technological independence and energy independence and negatively associated with all of the other indicators of dependency in order to be consistent with dependency theory.

Under the type of skewed associated dependent development which LDCs experience according to dependency theory, the installation of authoritarian regimes is a developmental prerequisite (Evans, 1983, p. 141). Evans argues that what makes dependent development possible is a "triple alliance" of state, multinational, and local capital. Otherwise, Evans argues that dependent development is a contradictory concept and dependency and development are opposites. Consequently, dependency theorists would expect greater GNP per capita under nondemocratic regimes. Dependency theorists also expect dependent development to carry the added cost of inequality (Cardoso and Faletto, 1979). Therefore, GNP per capita should be expected to be positively associated with inequality in order to be consistent with dependency theory. A synopsis of the findings regarding the GNP per capita variable are presented below in Table 5.5.

Table 5.5: Bivariate Relationships: GNP per Capita

Variable	r	Expected by dependency	Dependency support
Core trade	.23	Unexpected	Unsupportive
Trade concentration	***-.01**	**Expected**	**Very weak**
Debt % GNP	-.10	Unexpected	Unsupportive
Aid % GNP	***-.29**	**Expected**	**Supportive**
DFI % GNP	-.02	Unexpected	Unsupportive
Energy independence	.04	Unexpected	Unsupportive
Primary exports	***-.52**	**Expected**	**Supportive**
Technological independence	***.18**	**Expected**	**Supportive**
GNP	***.39**	**Unexpected**	**Unsupportive**
Population Growth	.05	Expected	Supportive
Area	.13	Expected	Supportive
Regime type	***.34**	**Unexpected**	**Unsupportive**
Inequality	.10	Unexpected	Unsupportive
PQLI	***.43**	**Unexpected**	**Unsupportive**
Quality Improvement	***-.19**	**Expected**	**Supportive**

*Significant at .05 level

The results of the bivariate correlations regarding GNP per capita are generally supportive of dependency expectations. GNP per capita exhibits statistically significant associations with   .de c ncentration, aid, primary exports, and technological independence, in the direction expected by dependency theory. No statistically significant relationships are observed between dependency indicators and GNP per capita which are contrary to the direction expected by dependency theory. Additionally, the relationships between GNP per capita and aid and primary exports are relatively strong (-.29 and -.52, respectively).

Despite this support for dependency theory, the results of the bivariate correlations alone do not provide enough evidence to conclude that dependency causes a lower GNP per capita. Obviously, the distinct possibility remains that the observed relationships are indeed spurious. If such is the case, then these relationships might no longer remain significant when the proper controls are implemented in multivariate analysis.

Dependency theory also receives tacit support through the lack of statistically significant relationships between GNP per capita and the control variables area and population growth. The lack of statistically significant relationships in these cases is supportive of the dependency position that underdevelopment in LDCs does not stem from internal causes such as these. Conversely, GNP per capita proves to be positively associated with GNP in a statistically significant (.39) correlation. This association suggests that GNP may be an important factor which could confound the observed relationships between dependency and GNP per capita when implemented as a control in multivariate analysis.

Similarly, the statistically significant positive (.34) association between GNP per capita and democratic regime types is difficult to explain under the dependency perspective. O'Donnell (1973) argues that LDCs must institute bureaucratic-authoritarian regimes in order to control the populist pressures created by dependent development. The observed positive relationship between GNP per capita and democratic regimes undermines this argument and, instead, is consistent with the liberal-modernization perspective of Lipset (1963) and Huntington (1990) who argue that democracy and wealth go hand in hand.

In a similar vein, the lack of a statistically significant relationship between GNP per capita and inequality is unexpected by the associated-dependent development thesis of Cardoso and Faletto (1979). According to this thesis, development in the dependent economies of LDCs carries with it the price of inequality. Support for this thesis is not observed. Furthermore, the strong statistically significant positive association between GNP per capita and PQLI appears to suggest that even if inequality does increase under dependent development (which was not observed), the betterment of the basic human condition does tend to be associated with higher GNP per capita.

GNP per capita is observed to be negatively (-.19) associated with PQLI growth (hereafter referred to as Quality Improvement). This finding is consistent with the associated-dependent development thesis which would expect conditions to worsen for the masses in LDCs as GNP per capita rises in structurally unbalanced dependent development. The possibility remains open, however, that this relationship is reflective of a law of diminishing returns on Improvement where it becomes more difficult to increase Improvement on a percentage basis as PQLI rises.

In general, the results of the bivariate analysis of GNP per capita are mixed. All of the dependency indicators that achieved statistical significance and Improvement exhibit relationships that are consistent with the dependency perspective while the control variables GNP, regime type, and PQLI produce associations which are inconsistent with dependency expectations.

Dependency and Growth

The results of the bivariate correlations involving dependency and GNP per capita growth are presented below in Table 5.6. Perhaps the most striking element of the results of the bivariate analysis regarding GNP per capita growth is the failure of all but two variables to achieve statistical significance.

Table 5.6: Bivariate Relationships: GNP per Capita Growth

Variable	r	Expected by dependency	dependency support
Core trade	.18	Unexpected	Unsupportive
Trade concentration	-.02	Unexpected	Unsupportive
Debt % GNP	-.19	Unexpected	Unsupportive
Aid % GNP	-.12	Unexpected	Unsupportive
DFI % GNP	0	Unexpected	Unsupportive
Energy independence	.06	Unexpected	Unsupportive
Primary exports	***-.22**	**Expected**	**Supportive**
Tech. independence	.08	Unexpected	Unsupportive
Population growth	-.02	Expected	Supportive
Area	-.03	Expected	Supportive
GNP	.15	Expected	Supportive
GNP per capita	***.27**	**Unexpected**	**Unsupportive**
Regime type	.07	Unexpected	Unsupportive
Inequality	-.07	Expected	Supportive
PQLI	.09	Unexpected	Unsupportive
Quality Improvement	-.07	Unexpected	Unsupportive

*Significant at .05 level

The only statistically significant dependency indicator associated with GNP per capita growth is primary export dependence; however, the -.22 correlation is in the direction consistent with dependency theory. This finding is particularly important since primary exports are also negatively associated with GNP per capita. The combination of the two findings provides support for the important "unequal exchange" thesis of dependency theory. Since this variable was also strongly negatively related to GNP per capita, the findings suggest that reliance on primary exports is related to both lower living standards and slower economic growth, leading to lower living standards. The possibility remains, however, that these observed relationships will disappear when controls are implemented in multivariate analysis. Conversely, if the relationship remains significant in multivariate analysis, then a central argument of dependency theory is supported.

Other than this GNP per capita growth/primary export association, however, the lack of statistically significant results suggests that dependency is largely unrelated to GNP per capita growth; therefore, the results are generally unsupportive of dependency theory. The only other statistically significant association that is observed regarding GNP per capita growth is a positive (.27) correlation with GNP per capita. This association is difficult to explain since mathematically one would expect states with lower GNP per capita to have greater potential for larger percentage growth.

For example, a state with a GNP per capita of $200 could grow 10 percent with an increase of only $20. The same $20 GNP per capita growth results in only 1 percent growth for states with GNP per capita of $2000. Since such small absolute increases result in large percentage increases in states with lower GNP per capita, it is perhaps surprising that GNP per capita and growth are positively related. The possibility remains, however, that this observed association will also disappear when proper controls are implemented in multivariate analysis.

The statistically insignificant results involving GNP per capita growth and the control variables population growth, area, and GNP can be interpreted as consistent with the dependency perspective since these are internal factors which dependency theorists would not expect to impact development. Conversely, the statistically insignificant relationships between GNP per capita growth and inequality and regime type are inconsistent with the theses of Cardoso and Faletto (1979) and Evans (1983). The lack of statistically significant relationships in these areas seriously undermine the new dependency theses. Similarly, no statistically significant relationships were observed between GNP per capita growth and PQLI or PQLI growth. In general, the income inequality (Cardoso and Faletto, 1979) and authoritarianism (Evans, 1983), which are presumed to accompany "associated dependent development," are not observed.

In general, the dependency perspective receives little support from the bivariate analysis involving GNP per capita growth, and different results are not expected through further analysis Despite this, multivariate analysis remains necessary for further investigation of the relationship between reliance on primary exports and GNP per capita growth, which is observed to be consistent with dependency theory in the bivariate analysis.

Dependency and Inequality

Similar to the results of the bivariate relationships involving GNP per capita growth, the results of the bivariate analysis involving inequality prove to be largely statistically insignificant. Also similar to the results involving GNP per capita growth, the only dependency variable which produces statistically significant results with inequality is reliance on primary exports. A pattern now appears to be developing regarding the primary export variable. Reliance on primary exports is observed to be positively (.25) associated with inequality. Reliance on primary exports is, therefore, associated with all three independent variables (GNP per capita, growth, and inequality) in the direction expected by the dependency perspective. Table 5.7 below provides a synopsis of the correlation results regarding dependency and inequality.

Table 5.7: Bivariate Relationships: Inequality

variable	r	Expected by dependency	Dependency support
Core trade	-.47	Unexpected	Unsupported
Trade concentration	.09	Unexpected	Unsupported
Debt % GNP	.06	Unexpected	Unsupported
Aid % GNP	.01	Unexpected	Unsupported
DFI % GNP	-.08	Unexpected	Unsupported
Energy independence	-.04	Unexpected	Unsupported
Primary export	***.25**	**Expected**	**Supportive**
Tech. independence	.07	Unexpected	Unsupported
Regime type	-.02	Unexpected	Unsupported
Population growth	.16	Expected	Supportive
Area	.23	Expected	Supportive
GNP	.04	Expected	Supportive
GNP per capita	.10	Unexpected	Unsupportive
GNP per ca. growth	-.07	Unexpected	Unsupported
PQLI	.10	Unexpected	Unsupportive
Quality Improvement	-.0	Unexpected	Unsupportive

*Significant at .05 level

Also similar to the results of the bivariate analysis involving growth, the three control variables GNP, area, and population growth are not significantly associated with inequality. Once again, the lack of statistical significance of these findings is consistent with dependency expectations regarding the impact of such internal factors on inequality. Despite this tacit support for dependency theory regarding the control variables, little support for dependency is produced by the dependency indicators themselves. Seven of the eight dependency indicators fail to produce statistically significant relationships with inequality. Furthermore, the negative associations expected by dependency theory between inequality and GNP per capita, GNP per capita growth, PQLI, and PQLI growth (Quality Improvement), do not emerge in a statistically significant fashion. Unfortunately, the lack of statistically significant results may be due to the small dataset (183 cases) rather than deficiencies in the dependency perspective. In this respect, the interpretation of the bivariate results involving inequality must remain inconclusive. In general, however, the results suggest that dependency may be of limited utility in explaining the inequality variable.

Dependency and PQLI

Dependency theorists would expect dependency to be negatively associated with PQLI. Implicit in this argument is that whatever development occurs in dependent economies, it is a skewed development which benefits only the wealthy and produces very few if any benefits for the masses (Chilcote and Edelstein, 1974). Table 5.8 below provides a synopsis of the relationship between the dependency variables and PQLI.

In general, the results are mixed with some relationships consistent with dependency theory while others are inconsistent. Of the relationships supportive of dependency theory, two results stand out. First, aid is strongly (-.46) negative in its association with PQLI as dependency theorists would predict. It remains possible, however, that aid does not contribute to lower PQLI, but is given by the industrialized core as a remedy for the already existing low PQLI in LDCs. It is logical to assume that low PQLI tends to attract aid from the core. Insight into the nature of the aid-PQLI relationship can be gained through the investigation of the relationship between aid and Quality Improvement.

Table 5.8: Bivariate Relationships: Dependency and PQLI

Variable	r	Expected by dependency	Dependency support
Core trade	.22	Unexpected	Unsupportive
Trade concentration	***.12**	**Unexpected**	**Unsupportive**
Debt % GNP	-.02	Unexpected	Unsupportive
Aid % GNP	***-.46**	**Expected**	**Supportive**
DFI % GNP	- 0	Unexpected	Unsupportive
Energy independence	-.02	Unexpected	Unsupportive
Primary export dep.	***-.35**	**Expected**	**Supportive**
Technological independence	.25	Unexpected	Unsupportive
Population growth	-.30	Expected	Supportive
Area	.01	Expected	Supportive
Regime	***.39**	**Expected**	**Supportive**
GNP	.25	Expected	Supportive
GNP per capita	***.43**	**Unexpected**	**Unsupportive**
GNP per capita growth	.09	Unexpected	Unsupportive
Inequality	.10	Unexpected	Unsupportive
Quality Improvement	***-.45**	**Unexpected**	**Unsupportive**

*Significant at .05 level

If aid proves to be positively associated with Quality Improvement, then it is logically inferred that aid is likely the result of, rather than the cause of, low PQLI. If such is the case, then dependency theorists have confused the causal order of the aid/PQLI relationship. Multivariate analysis should be useful for revealing the character of this relationship by holding PQLI constant when investigating the relationship between aid and Quality Improvement.

A second relationship, which is strongly in the direction expected by dependency theory, is the negative (-.35) association between reliance on primary exports and PQLI. The behavior of the primary export variable is consistent with the dependency perspective in its association with all four of the dependent variables analyzed. Hence, no results require rejection of the unequal exchange thesis; however, the mere negative association between primary exports and PQLI does not infer causation. Greater insight into the causal nature of the relationship can be gained through the analysis of the dependency indicators and Quality Improvement. Furthermore, it remains possible that the control variables are factors which confound the relationships and the observed negative association between primary exports and PQLI might disappear when controls are included in the analysis.

Other findings which support the dependency perspective are the statistically insignificant relationships between PQLI and the control variables GNP, area, and population growth. Since all of these represent internal rather than external factors, dependency theorists would not expect them to be of value for explaining PQLI.

Democratic regimes do exhibit a statistically significant positive (.39) association with PQLI. This finding is consistent with classic liberal theory (Snider, 1971; Ellsworth, 1969; Schumpeter, 1942) which views democracy and capitalism as working together for the benefit of all society. Democratic regimes are also positively associated (.34) with GNP per capita consistent with the modernization arguments of Lipset (1963) and Schumpeter (1942). The positive relationship between democratic regimes and GNP per capita, perhaps, increases the probability that the democracy/PQLI relationship will disappear when GNP per capita is held constant in multivariate analysis. GNP per capita is also positively (.43) associated with PQLI, a finding which is inconsistent with dependency theory since it infers that, not only the upper class but also the lower class may be benefiting from the aggregate wealth of the state.

A number of other relationships are observed which are unsupportive of dependency theory. One dependency indicator, trade concentration, is positively (.12) associated with PQLI suggesting that the lower classes in LDCs may not be suffering from exploitive core-periphery trade relationships. Additionally, trade with the core, debt, direct foreign investment, energy independence, and technological independence all fail to produce statistically significant correlations. This lack of significant relationships is inconsistent with the dependency perspective which expects all of these factors to have deleterious effects on PQLI. Consequently, the usefulness of dependency for explaining PQLI appears to be questionable based on the results of the bivariate analysis.

Finally, no statistically significant relationship between PQLI and inequality is observed; consequently, the inference of dependency theorists that physical quality of life in LDCs suffers from dependency-induced inequality is unsupported. Also unsupported is the dependency inference that economic growth in LDCs is skewed and benefits the upper classes at the expense of the lower.

In general, the results of the bivariate analysis involving PQLI were mixed, with dependency supported in some cases and unsupported in others. Investigation of the relationships between dependency and PQLI growth is necessary to gain a better understanding of the relationships between aid and reliance on primary exports and PQLI since it is in these areas that dependency theory receives its strongest support. Multivariate analysis will also be necessary in order to determine if the observed dependency/PQLI associations continue to hold when proper controls are introduced.

Dependency and Quality Improvement

Table 5.9 contains the results of the bivariate analysis involving PQLI growth (Quality Improvement). Similar to the results of bivariate analysis of the other dependent variables, the majority of the dependency indicators do not produce statistically significant associations with Quality Improvement, suggesting that these dependency indicators may be of limited utility for explaining Quality Improvement. The lack of statistically significant associations between the majority of the dependency indicators and Quality Improvement is unsupportive of the dependency perspective since dependency is hypothesized to produce "underdevelopment."

Perhaps most important is the failure of primary export dependence to produce a statistically significant association with Quality Improvement. This is particularly important since primary export dependence is negatively associated with PQLI and all of the other dependent variables utilized in this study. The results suggest that although primary export dependence may be associated with low PQLI, it may not be a factor that perpetuates low PQLI or hinders quality improvement. This finding is inconsistent with the unequal exchange argument of dependency theorists.

In contrast to these statistically insignificant results, the strongest statistically significant association (aid and Quality Improvement) produces a positive .26 correlation which is contradictory to dependency expectations. If this association remains strong when proper controls are introduced in multivariate analysis, then dependency theory will be seriously undermined. In essence, the association is supportive of the liberal policy prescription for meeting basic human needs in LDCs through aid. The association suggests that aid may benefit a broad segment of the population rather than the upper class international bourgeoisie as dependency theorists contend. The positive association between aid and Quality Improvement suggests that the negative relationship between aid and PQLI is best explained as a situation where states suffering from low PQLI tend to attract aid from the core, in turn contributing to Quality Improvement. Multivariate analysis with proper controls implemented is needed to confirm this possibility.

Table 5.9: Bivariate Relationships: Quality Improvement

Variable	r	Expected by dependency	Dependency support
Core trade	-.09	Unexpected	Unsupportive
Trade concentration	*-.13	**Expected**	**Supportive**
Debt % GNP	.02	Unexpected	Unsupportive
Aid % GNP	* .26	**Unexpected**	**Unsupportive**
DFI % GNP	.03	Unexpected	Unsupportive
Energy independence	* .17	**Expected**	**Supportive**
Primary export dependence	.15	Unexpected	Unsupportive
Technological independence	-.14	Unexpected	Unsupportive
Population growth	.17	Expected	Supportive
Area	-.03	Expected	Supportive
GNP	-.13	Expected	Supportive
Regime	-.18	Unexpected	Unsupportive
GNP per capita	*-.19	**Expected**	**Supportive**
GNP per capita growth	-.07	Unexpected	Unsupportive
Inequality	0	Unexpected	Unsupportive
PQLI	*-.45	**Unexpected**	**Unsupportive**

*Significant at .05 level

Trade partner concentration and energy independence produce statistically significant associations with Quality Improvement that are consistent with dependency expectations (-.13 and .17, respectively). In the case of trade concentration, the explanation for the observed relationship may lie outside of dependency theory. As previously discussed, trade partner concentration is positively (.12) associated with PQLI, which is in turn negatively associated with Quality Improvement. Consequently, the observed negative relationship between trade concentration and Quality Improvement may disappear when PQLI is controlled for in multivariate analysis.

Area, population growth, and GNP fail to produce statistically significant relationships with Quality Improvement. These findings are consistent with dependency expectations since dependency places emphasis on external factors rather than internal factors when explaining economic development. The failure of the regime variable to produce statistically significant associations with Quality Improvement is not easily explained by either the liberal or dependency perspectives since both generally infer that Quality Improvement should be greater under democratic regimes. It remains possible, however, (though not necessarily expected) that the regime variable may become important when controls are introduced.

Similar to the regime variable, inequality does not produce a statistically significant correlation with Quality Improvement. This finding is also contradictory to the expectations of the associated dependent development thesis of Cardoso and Faletto (1979) who infer that inequality has deleterious effects on Quality Improvement.

In sum, the results of the bivariate analysis tend to suggest that dependency may be of little utility for explaining Quality Improvement. Only two dependency indicators are associated with Quality Improvement in the direction expected by dependency theory and those relationships may disappear when proper controls are included in multivariate analysis. Furthermore, aid is positively related to Quality Improvement, contrary to the dependency argument. Finally, the strong negative associations between Quality Improvement and PQLI and GNP per capita suggest that PQLI and GNP per capita may be of greater utility in explaining Improvement than any indicators of dependency.

Summary: Bivariate Analysis

Factor analysis revealed that dependency is a multidimensional concept since the variables load on three factors; however, the factors will not be used in further analysis due to difficulties in the interpretation of the factors, which are somewhat more ambiguous than the dependency indicators themselves.

From bivariate correlations between all of the independent, control, and dependent variables, a number of general patterns emerged. First, the majority of the relationships between the dependency indicators and the dependent variables are statistically insignificant. Second, the direction of the relationships between some of the dependency indicators and the dependent variables are opposite to dependency expectations. Third, strong associations are present between a number of the dependent variables and control variables. These associations suggest that the control variables may be important factors that may confound the relationships produced through bivariate analysis when included as controls in multivariate analysis. In general, dependency appears to be of limited utility in explaining the dependent variables. Multivariate analysis with proper controls is needed to confirm or invalidate this conclusion.

Chapter 6

Dependency, Wealth, and Growth

In the following sections, the independent variables are regressed on the dependent variables GNP per capita and GNP per capita growth in a series of pooled multiple regressions in order to determine how much of the variance the selected dependency indicators are able to explain in each of the dependent variables. It is important to investigate the relationships between the dependency indicators and the dependent variables, both with and without the control variables, in order to gain insight into what proportion of the variance the respective dependency indicators and control variables explain.

The chapter proceeds as follows: Descriptive statistics are presented and discussed for each dependent variable prior to statistical manipulation. Subsequent sections empirically investigate the relationships between dependency indicators and GNP per capita (wealth) and GNP per capita growth respectively with and without control variables through pooled time series multivariate analysis. The final section is a summary and conclusions.

We include a presentation of descriptive statistics in order to assist in drawing conclusions from the data analysis which follows. In the case of GNP per capita, the descriptive statistics provide insight into the extent of poverty in LDCs as well as the great diversity within LDCs. In the multivariate analysis, we control for all of the other dependency variables when investigating each independent variable since the bivariate analysis indicated some inter-relatedness which may confound the relationships between the dependency indicators and the dependent variables. The multivariate analysis should provide insight into the relative importance of each dependency indicator in regard to the other aspects of dependency.

The analysis may yield a number of different results. First, it is possible that all of the findings may indicate strong relationships in the direction predicted by dependency theory. If so, then we can say that the dependency perspective has withstood fairly difficult cross-national tests regarding wealth and growth. Second, it is possible that the independent variables selected to tap dependency might be largely unrelated to either wealth or growth. Such findings would suggest that dependency is of little use in predicting wealth or growth in LDCs. Third, it is possible that all of the findings will indicate strong relationships in the direction that is contrary to the dependency perspective. In other words, though the concept of dependency carries an overwhelmingly negative connotation in dependency literature, the results may suggest that dependency, on the contrary, may be positively related to wealth and growth in LDCs. If such is the case, then dependency may be a very useful concept for explaining the variance in growth and wealth in LDCs as dependency theorists contend, but the dependency position that dependency is negatively associated with wealth and growth would be contradicted.

Fourth, it is possible that support for dependency will be mixed, with dependency supported by some relationships and unsupported by others. In such a case, the results are inconclusive and the significance of the findings are more difficult to interpret. A mix of strong negative and strong positive relationships may produce a healthy R2, yet provide little insight into the overall directional impact of dependency on the dependent variables. In such a case, the results would suggest that dependency theory does have some merit in some areas, but is perhaps less holistic and all inclusive than dependency theorists (Caporaso, 1980; Duvall, 1978) have suggested, and in need of revision. It should be noted that a positive relationship between dependency and growth would not be inconsistent with the associated dependent development thesis of Cardoso and Faletto (1979). For this reason, the relationships between dependency and inequality and PQLI must be investigated in subsequent chapters. A negative relationship between dependency and inequality and a positive relationship between dependency and PQLI growth would be particularly damaging to their arguments. This discussion is reflective of the fact that the number of individual relationships to be observed is quite substantial and may produce results which are complex in nature and elude simplistic interpretation. In all probability, the results may not produce an outright acceptance or rejection of the dependency perspective as such, but it is hoped that it will produce significant insight into the relationship between dependency and growth, inequality, and Physical Quality of Life which will lead to further exploration of these relationships in the future.

Data Analysis: GNP per Capita

Descriptive statistics regarding GNP per capita are presented below in Table 6.1. With a standard deviation of almost fifteen hundred dollars and a range of over fourteen thousand dollars, there is a good deal of variance in wealth among LDCs as was to be expected. Dependency may be useful in explaining this variance based upon the results of the bivariate analysis where four of the eight dependency indicators (trade concentration, aid, primary exports, and technological independence) were significant in the direction expected by dependency theory. The possibility remains, however, that the observed significant bivariate relationships might fail to remain observable when controls are implemented.

Although some, and perhaps even most, dependency indicators may produce a strong negative relationship with GNP per capita, dependency theorists cannot rule out the possibility that these relationships are produced in a causal order opposite to that of dependency theory. As previously discussed, it is likely that aid will exhibit a negative relationship with GNP per capita; however, this negative association may be due to aid donations from the core as a response to the already existing low periphery GNP per capita rather than due to a causal relationship where aid is producing low GNP per capita. In other words, poverty may be attracting aid rather than aid producing poverty.

Table 6.1 GNP Per Capita Statistics

Valid cases	445
Mean	1008.386
Standard Deviation	1488.375
Minimum	50
Maximum	14340

Pooled Regressions: GNP Per Capita

The results of the first pooled regression utilizing the GLS-ARMA method dealing with the relationship between dependency and GNP per capita without controls are presented below in Table 6.2. All of the basic regression statistics are reported along with their significance level (d=.05). If the B coefficients predict a relationship in the direction expected by the dependency perspective, they are designated as "expected." If the direction indicated by the B coefficients are inconsistent with the dependency perspective, they are designated as "unexpected." Those variables which failed to achieve statistical significance are also designated as expected or unexpected.

Table 6.2 Dependency and GNP per Capita: No Controls

Variable	B	Standard Error	t	sig. .05	Expected by dependency
Constant	2078.34	201.903	10.293	yes	
Core Trade	1.5519	2.2033	0.7043	no	Unexpected
Trade Concen.	-48.457	43.3931	-1.1167	no	Unexpected
Debt %GNP	0.1170	1.0061	0.1162	no	Unexpected
Aid %GNP	-11.412	6.7285	-1.6962	no	Unexpected
DFI%GNP	-0.5615	1.2505	-0.4491	no	Unexpected
Patents	0.0943	0.0533	1.7704	no	Unexpected
Energy Dep.	-2.3560	2.0633	-1.1419	no	Unexpected
Primary Exp.	**-17.695**	**2.2214**	**-7.9658**	**yes**	**Expected**

Adjusted R2=.15   Pooled Durbin-Watson D: .99

The results of the pooled regression between the dependency indicators and GNP per capita without controls do not, for the most part, conform to the tenets of dependency theory. Over 84 percent of the variance in GNP per capita remains unexplained and seven of the eight dependency variables failed to achieve statistical significance. Hence, at first glance, dependency appears to be largely unrelated to GNP per capita in LDCs. Furthermore, the statistically significant relationships observed in bivariate correlations between GNP per capita and aid, trade concentration, and technological independence all fail to surface in the multivariate analysis when all of the other dependency variables are held constant.

On the other hand, the results regarding primary exports which were supportive of dependency theory in the bivariate analysis proved to be also consistent with dependency theory in multivariate analysis. The B coefficient for this variable reveals that a one percent increase in nonfuel primary products as a percentage of exports is associated with a GNP per capita, which is lower by $17.69.

Though this finding is consistent with the dependency perspective, it is also consistent with the liberal paradigm which stresses the development of other portions of the export sector of the economy besides raw material exports. Finally, when other factors, such as population growth are held constant, it is possible that this observed relationship may vanish. It is also possible that the other dependency indicators may be significant factors in explaining GNP per capita, but the relationships are obscured without proper controls. Hence, it is necessary to include controls with the dependency indicators in the multivariate analysis. This analysis is reported in the following section. In closing, it should be mentioned that the pooled regression produced a Durbin-Watson statistic (.99) which is within the acceptable range (between 2 and -1) and indicates that problems of autocorrelation are within tolerance.

Pooled Regression with Controls: GNP per Capita

The results of the pooled regression between dependency and GNP per capita with controls implemented are presented below in Table 6.3. The dependency indicators combine with the control variables to explain over thirty percent of the variance in GNP per capita among LDCs over the twenty-six year period under analysis. This relatively strong R^2 (.31) was not unexpected based on the results of the correlation analysis and the pooled regression results without controls; however, since dependency without controls explained only .15 percent of the variance, a large portion of the variance explained in the analysis when the controls are included may be attributable to the control variables.

Again, only one dependency variable (reliance on nonfuel primary products in exports) achieved statistical significance when all of the others were held constant. This finding was unexpected both by dependency theorists and by this researcher. Still, the findings are not without substantive significance.

The direction of the one dependency variable which was statistically significant proved to be consistent with dependency theory. Namely, the B coefficient revealed that for every one percent increase in nonfuel primary products as a percentage of exports, GNP per capita tended to be less by an increment of $9.70. Though this figure proved to be less (as expected) than the results for dependency without controls, the finding must still be considered as some substantively significant support for dependency theory.

Table 6.3: Dependency and GNP per Capita

Variable	B	Standard Error	t	sig. .05	Expected by dependency
Constant	1208.75	258.9161	4.6685	yes	
Core Trade	1.2591	1.9946	0.6312	no	Unexpected
Trade Concen.	-63.003	39.9710	-1.5762	no	Unexpected
Debt %GNP	-0.4369	0.8993	-0.4858	no	Unexpected
Aid %GNP	-9.0589	6.0514	-1.4970	no	Unexpected
DFI%GNP	-0.3315	1.1320	-0.2928	no	Unexpected
Patents	-0.0634	0.0519	-1.2219	no	Unexpected
Energy Dep.	-1.0009	1.8368	-05449	no	Unexpected
Primary Exp.	**-9.7054**	**2.1828**	**-4.4462**	**yes**	**Expected**
GNP	**0.0167**	**0.0017**	**9.7464**	**yes**	**Unexpected**
Pop Growth	78.3312	50.1127	1.5631	no	Expected
Area	**-0.0003**	**0.0001**	**-3.9303**	**yes**	**Unexpected**
Inequality	8.6419	9.6462	0.8959	no	Unexpected
Regime Type	**361.971**	**145.5915**	**2.4862**	**yes**	**Unexpected**

Adjusted R^2=.31   Pooled Durbin-Watson D: .88

Once again, however, the statistically significant relationships reported in bivariate analysis between GNP per capita and the dependency indicators trade concentration, aid, and technological independence do not hold in the multivariate analysis, suggesting that the statistically significant bivariate relationships are spurious.

The results of the statistically significant control variables in the multivariate analysis are counter to dependency theory. Perhaps most important, the democracies possessed GNP per capitas which were $361.97 larger than non-democracies when all of the other variables were held constant. This finding appears to conflict with the dependency argument (Cardoso, 1973, p. 172) that dependent LDCs could only develop through the implementation of authoritarian regimes. In the words of Cardoso (1973, p. 176), "any technical formula for mass mobilization will lead to mass manipulation, and perhaps to an increase in the accumulation of wealth, but will not bring about political development favoring the majority and increasing the quality of life." Additionally, Cardoso (1973, p. 172) acknowledges that there is a prevalent notion among dependency theorists that economic growth and authoritarianism are inextricably linked. Once again, in the words of Cardoso (1973, p. 172),

> This association between an increased growth rate and author-
> itarianism has encouraged the notion that they bear an intimate and

necessary relation to each other. In this view, authoritarianism is seen
as a prerequisite for economic development.

The finding that democracies had higher GNP per capita when all of the other
variables are held constant is much more consistent with the modernization
position of Lipset (1959, 1963), who contends that there is a positive association
between the development of democratic regimes and economic prosperity, than
with dependency theory.

The dependent variable area also achieved statistical significance, basically
in contradiction with the position of the dependency perspective that
development within LDCs is determined by external factors (Bath and James,
1976); however, the B coefficient which was produced for area was quite small,
indicating that an increase of 100,000 square miles of area is associated with a
GNP per capita decrease of $30.00. Hence, the substantive significance of area
in explaining the variance in GNP per capita is questionable.

In sum, the results of the data analysis are neither overwhelmingly
supportive, nor completely disparaging of the proposition that dependency has
an adverse effect on GNP per capita. Although the failure of the majority of the
dependency variables to achieve statistical significance in multivariate analysis
is disappointing in that it was unexpected by both dependency theory and the
hypotheses presented here, the findings are not without utility. Importantly, the
low R2 and failure to reach statistical significance of the dependency indicators
suggest that other factors not included in the analysis are more important for
explaining development in LDCs than dependency.

Of the dependency indicators, only reliance on primary exports appears to
be associated with lower per capita income. Greater understanding of the nature
of this relationship can be gained through the multivariate analysis of the
relationship between the dependency indicators and economic growth. If
reliance on primary exports proves to be also negatively related to economic
growth when all other factors are held constant, then an important element of
dependency theory retains support through rigorous empirical analysis.
Conversely, if primary exports proves to be either unrelated or positively related
to economic growth, then the dependency position that reliance on primary
exports produces "underdevelopment" is unsupported.

Data Analysis: Economic Growth

Data are readily available for growth as represented by annual percentage
change in GNP per capita for LDCs. Four hundred forty-five of the possible four
hundred sixty-two cases are recorded for this variable. Presented below in Table
6.4 are the relevant descriptive statistics for the dependent variable growth.

The descriptive statistics for growth reveal a wide range for growth among
LDCs from the -13.7 percent for Nicaragua from 1988-1992 to the positive 46.3
percent for Trinidad and Tobago from 1978-1982. Perhaps most importantly, the
seventy-seven countries averaged an annual growth rate of 3.85 percent over the

twenty-six year period. This robust growth rate presents problems for radical dependency theorists who would not expect such growth due to the dependent status of these LDCs. Dependency simply did not prevent robust growth on the average for the countries studied during this time period.

Table 6.4 GNP per Capita Growth Statistics

Valid cases	445
Missing cases	17
Mean	3.85%
Standard Deviation	7.56
Minimum	-13.7
Maximum	46.3

Pooled Regressions: Economic Growth

Below the results of the multiple regressions involving the independent variables representing dependency and GNP per capita growth are presented in Table 6.5. The results for the pooled regression involving dependency and growth without controls are again largely unsupportive of the dependency perspective. The pooled regression produced an R2 of only .15 which suggests that 85 percent of the variance in growth is explained by factors other than dependency. Furthermore, the pooled Durbin-Watson D statistic of 2.45 reveals that some correlation of the error terms is present, hence that R2 may be unreliable and suggest that dependency explains more of the variance than it actually does. Consequently, dependency may not even account for as much as the 15 percent of the variance indicated. Additionally, four of the eight dependency variables failed to achieve statistical significance, and two variables, core trade and trade concentration, achieved statistical significance in the direction which is counter to the expectations of the dependency perspective. If the apparent statistical significance of these two trade variables is valid, then these findings strike a serious blow to the dependency perspective. Essentially, radical dependency theorists cannot explain how increased trade with the core and increased concentration of trade in one or two trading partners could contribute to growth in LDCs. Furthermore, the B coefficient for the concentration variable suggests that a one percent increase in concentration of trade in the top two core trading partners as a percentage of total trade is associated with a growth rate which is increased by .84 percent. Obviously, trade partner concentration may have an important positive role in fostering growth in LDCs. Two variables, debt as a percentage of GNP and reliance on primary exports, appear to be associated with slower growth as predicted by the dependency perspective.

Perhaps most important are the results regarding reliance on primary exports since it was also associated with low GNP per capita as well as slower growth. The B coefficient for primary exports suggests that a 10 percent increase in primary exports as a percentage of exports is associated with a decrease in GNP per capita growth by .3 percent when all of the other dependency indicators are held constant. Consequently, consistent with the arguments of the dependency perspective, reliance on primary exports appears to be negatively related to both GNP per capita and GNP per capita growth, therefore contributing both to poverty and slower economic growth. Further analysis is necessary to determine if the relationship remains significant when the proper controls are implemented.

Table 6.5 Dependency and Growth: No Controls

Variable	B	Standard Error	t	sig. .05	Expected by dependency	Expected by hypothesis 1
Constant	4.6872	0.8071	5.8078	yes		
Core Trade	**0.0515**	**0.0116**	**4.4517**	**yes**	**Unexpected**	**Expected**
Trade Concen.	**0.8447**	**0.1822**	**4.6365**	**yes**	**Unexpected**	**Expected**
Debt %GNP	**-0.0202**	**0.0053**	**-3.8059**	**yes**	**Expected**	**Unexpected**
Aid %GNP	-0.0060	0.0355	-0.1684	no	Unexpected	Unexpected
DFI%GNP	0.0025	0.0055	0.4465	no	Unexpected	Unexpected
Patents	0.0004	0.0003	1.4524	no	Unexpected	Unexpected
Energy Dep.	0.0099	0.0116	0.8578	no	Unexpected	Unexpected
Primary Exp.	**-0.0307**	**0.0094**	**-3.2623**	**yes**	**Expected**	**Unexpected**

Adjusted R2=.15   Pooled Durbin-Watson D: 2.45

Debt as a percentage of GNP appears to be statistically significant in the direction predicted by the dependency perspective. Hence, when the other dependency indicators are controlled for, a negative relationship emerges between debt and economic growth which was not statistically significant in the bivariate analysis. Though this relationship is consistent with the dependency perspective, it should be noted that the negative relationship between debt and growth is also consistent with liberal expectations. Essentially, the liberal economic perspective expects a negative relationship between debt and growth since resources that are funneled into debt service are not put into investment which stimulates growth. Further analysis with controls implemented is needed in order to better understand the nature of this relationship.

Finally, though some support for the dependency position does appear to emerge from the data analysis, especially on the primary exports variable, these relationships may not remain significant when proper controls are implemented. Furthermore, the statistically significant relationships may fail to materialize if the autocorrelation is eliminated. Consequently, the results of the pooled regression involving dependency and GNP per capita growth with controls are presented below in Table 6.6 It is hoped that the problem of the autocorrelation will be corrected with the introduction of the control variables. If the autocorrelation persists after the introduction of the control variables, then other measures will be introduced in efforts to achieve its elimination.

Pooled Regression with Controls: Economic Growth

As shown in Table 6.6, the results provided little support for the hypothesis that dependency is positively related to GNP per capita growth. The pooled regression produced a low R2 which left over 83 percent of the variance unexplained by dependency and the control variables. In this case, the control variables appear to be of limited use for explaining the variance in GNP per capita growth since the R2 of .166 achieved with control variables amounts to little change from the .15 R2 without control variables. Furthermore, only two control variables, GNP per capita and area, achieved statistical significance.

Despite this limited contribution of the control variables in explaining the variance in GNP per capita growth, their utility is well illustrated by the changes in reliance on primary exports. This variable, which appeared to have significant impact on GNP per capita growth when controls were not introduced, becomes insignificant when the control variables are added. Hence, this evidence suggests that the previously observed association between primary exports and GNP per capita growth in multivariate analysis is a spurious relationship which disappears when proper controls are introduced. In sum, though reliance on primary exports may be important in explaining GNP per capita, it is not a significant factor in explaining economic growth.

Table 6.6: Dependency and Growth with Controls

Variable	B	Standard Error	t	sig. .05	Expected by dependency	Expected by hypothesis 1
Constant	3.0950	1.1031	2.8057	yes		
Core Trade	**0.0440**	**0.0120**	**3.6678**	**yes**	**Unexpected**	**Expected**
Trade Con.	**0.8279**	**0.1866**	**4.4362**	**yes**	**Unexpected**	**Expected**
Debt %GNP	**-0.0205**	**0.0053**	**-3.8391**	**yes**	**Expected**	**Unexpected**
Aid %GNP	0.0041	0.0360	0.1132	no	Unexpected	Unexpected
DFI%GNP	0.0038	0.0055	0.6935	no	Unexpected	Unexpected
Patents	0.0003	0.0003	0.9658	no	Unexpected	Unexpected
Energy Dep.	0.0151	0.0117	1.2868	no	Unexpected	Unexpected
Primary Exp.	-0.0116	0.0107	-1.0837	no	Unexpected	Unexpected
GNP	0.0000	0.0000	1.8050	no	Expected	Unexpected
Pop Growth	0.0621	0.2099	0.2958	no	Expected	Unexpected
Area	**-0.0000**	**0.0000**	**-2.4047**	**yes**	**Expected**	**Unexpected**
GNP per ca.	**0.0006**	**0.0002**	**2.7453**	**yes**	**Unexpected**	**Expected**
Regime Type	0.2608	0.7685	0.3393	no	Unexpected	Unexpected

Adjusted R2=.17   Pooled Durbin-Watson D: 2.43

Similar to the results regarding the relationship between dependency and GNP per capita growth without controls, the pooled Durbin-Watson D statistic of 2.43 suggests that autocorrelation is present; consequently, the reliability of the results from the analysis is questionable. The implication of autocorrelation is that the estimated regression line tends to fit the data better than it normally would (Ostrom, 1991, p. 22). If autocorrelation is indeed present in this case, then more reliable results, which might be achieved if autocorrelation were eliminated, would only confirm to an even greater degree what the results in Table 6.6 appear to suggest. In other words, the results suggest that dependency is of little utility in explaining GNP per capita growth since over 83 percent of the variance remains unexplained. If the R2 is higher than it should be due to autocorrelation, then the value of dependency in explaining growth is reduced even further. Either way, dependency appears to be largely unrelated to growth.

Additionally, the number of time points evaluated in the analysis (six) is relatively small in relation to the number of countries (seventy-seven). Nerlove (1971) and Stimson (1985) argue that in such cases autocorrelation is "more of a nuisance than a threat, and other considerations should dominate" (Stimson, 1985, p. 927). At any rate, Stimson (1985, p. 926) argues that autocorrelation is frequently a small problem relative to unit effects, and therefore scholars often have tended to "assume" it to the sidelines. We intend to "assume" autocorrelation to the sidelines only if it proves to be impossible to correct.

In order to correct for autocorrelation, Stimson (1985) suggests adding dummy variables for each unit in the analysis for which the residual variance ratio, a ratio of actual to expected variation in each unit, does not approximate zero. A review of the residual variance ratios for each case (see Appendix B) reveals that twenty-three countries produced scores over 1.0 or less than negative 1.0. Consequently, dummy variables were added for all twenty three countries and the GLS-ARMA procedure re-employed in an attempt to eliminate the autocorrelation. Countries with residual variance ratios over 1.0 are coded as one, and all others are coded as zero and included in the multivariate analysis. The pooled Durbin-Watson D statistic which was produced from this procedure was almost unchanged, and actually a less-favorable 2.46. Since Stimson (1985) argues that the success of this procedure in correcting autocorrelation is related to what degree that time points are dominant in relation to units, the fact that the addition of dummy variables was unable to eliminate the problem of autocorrelation is likely to be related to the large number of units (seventy-seven) as compared to time points (six). Consequently, since the autocorrelation cannot be eliminated in this case, we have little alternative but to note Stimson's (1985) argument that the autocorrelation in such cases is more of a "nuisance" than a problem and follow Stimson's suggestion that the autocorrelation problem be "assumed to the sidelines" while interpreting the results presented in Table 6.6.

Conclusions based on these results are not entirely without bases. Since the percentage of the variance which was explained was small, and the number of time points (six) as compared to units (seventy-seven) was also small, we argue that we have a good case for "assuming" autocorrelation to the sidelines. It must, however, be acknowledged that one of the consequences of autocorrelation may be unreliable t-scores and confidence levels (Ostrom,

1991). Therefore, we proceed with the analysis of the data with a reasonable degree of caution.

Three dependency indicators (trade with the core, trade partner concentration, and debt as a percentage of GNP) appear to be significant, with the first two exhibiting a relationship with GNP per capita growth in the direction consistent with hypothesis #1 (that dependency is positively related to growth) and the latter exhibiting a relationship consistent with the dependency perspective. The B coefficient for Trade with the core as a percentage of GNP suggests that every one percent change in Trade with the core as a percentage of GNP was associated with a .04% change in GNP per capita growth. This finding is consistent with the modernization perspective and suggests that increased trade with the core is a sound policy choice for LDCs which desire to increase GNP per capita growth.

Having even greater positive impact on growth than core trade as a percentage of GNP, appears to be trade partner concentration. The B coefficients indicate that a one percent increase in concentration of trade with the top two trading partners as a percentage of total trade is associated with a .83 percent increase in GNP per capita growth. This finding is clearly antithetical to the dependency perspective and suggests that concentrated trade relationships (which dependency theorists term as exploitive patron-client relationships) between core and periphery are beneficial to periphery growth rather than detrimental.

The one dependency variable, debt, that is negatively associated with growth as expected by the dependency perspective is also posited to be negatively related to growth by liberal theorists (Friedman, 1982, pp. 76-84). The B coefficient suggests that a one percent increase in debt as a percentage of GNP is associated with a GNP per capita growth that is slower by .02 percent. Hence, as a whole, debt "dependency" appears to be a hindrance to growth.

As previously mentioned, the control variables, as a whole, appear to be insignificant factors in explaining growth when all of the other factors were held constant. Only two control variables, GNP per capita and area, produced results which appear to be statistically significant. Perhaps surprisingly, a one thousand dollar increase in GNP per capita appears to be associated with a higher GNP per capita growth rate by .6 percent. In other words, when all of the other factors are held constant, wealthier LDCs can be expected to grow at a faster rate than poorer LDCs. The control variable area appears to be statistically significant, but with a B coefficient of zero, it does not appear to be useful for explaining the variance in GNP per capita growth.

Of the statistically insignificant variables, it is worth noting that regime type did not achieve statistical significance; hence the "new dependency" proposition that LDCs grow at a more rapid rate under authoritarian regimes is unsupported through multivariate analysis. Also important is the fact that the only dependency variable, primary exports, which produced statistical significance in the investigation of dependency and GNP per capita was statistically insignificant in explaining growth of GNP per capita. As a consequence, the dependency emphasis on the detrimental effect of reliance on raw materials in exports is unsupported.

In sum, while the results neither explain much of the variance in growth nor are supportive of Hypothesis #1, it is noteworthy that they are equally unsupportive of the radical dependency proposition that dependency hinders growth in LDCs. On the contrary, the results (which include an extremely low R2, statistical insignificance of five of the eight dependency variables, and mixed directional impact of the three significant variables) suggest that dependency is largely unrelated to growth in LDCs, and that most of growth in LDCs during this time period is explained by other factors unaccounted for by this equation. This finding in and of itself may be the most significant since it is contrary to the tenets of radical dependency theory.

The results pose several difficult questions for the dependency perspective. First, how is it possible that core states could construct exploitive, neocolonial trade relationships with LDCs if core trade as a percentage of GNP and core trade partner concentration are statistically significant factors which are associated positively with growth? Second, how could nonfuel primary products as a percentage of total exports fail to achieve statistical significance since this variable taps into the supposed root cause of "unequal exchange," the reliance on exports of raw materials, which supposedly is a major contributor to underdevelopment. Third, how could it be explained under dependency theory that aid and direct foreign investment, which tap into the concept of "capital dependency," failed to achieve statistical significance? Fourth, how can the statistical insignificance of the number of patents (which represents technological dependency) and energy production as a percentage of consumption (which represents energy dependency) be explained through dependency theory? The inference is that dependency is a meaningless concept for the purposes of explaining growth in LDCs.

Finally, it should be noted that the other two control variables, GNP and population growth, failed to achieve statistical significance. This finding is consistent with the dependency perspective since dependency theorists tend to view growth as externally caused; and therefore, these internal factors are expected to be insignificant by dependency theorists. These findings did not, however, lend support to the dependency perspective contention that dependency depresses growth. Instead the results merely fail to support the position that these control variables were significant factors in determining growth.

In general, dependency propositions regarding dependency and growth have been unsupported as has the hypothesis #1 position that dependency is positively related to growth. The statistical insignificance of all but three variables, the multi-directional nature of the relationships, and the anemic R2 observed, infer that attention should be devoted to factors other than dependency for the purpose of explaining growth in GNP per capita. Factors unaccounted for by dependency such as culture and geography may play a significant role in explaining the variance in growth. With little support uncovered thus far either for the dependency perspective, or for hypothesis #1, we proceed with the analysis of the relationship between dependency and inequality.

The analysis of inequality is necessary due to the "new dependency" arguments of Cardoso (1973) and Cardoso and Faletto (1979). In these works, the scholars argue that there is a range of possibilities for economic growth in dependent states and robust growth rates are possible; however, growth in dependent economies is not possible without increasing income inequalities. Hence, the analysis of wealth and growth is not a test of the associated dependent development thesis of "new dependency" theory, but only a test of the radical dependency perspective. Analysis of the relationship between the dependency indicators and inequality is required in order to test the "new dependency" argument.

Chapter 7

Dependency and Inequality

In this chapter, the relationship between the dependency indicators and inequality is investigated in a series of pooled regressions. First, descriptive statistics for inequality are presented followed by the presentation of the results of the pooled multiple regressions linking modes of external dependence to inequality. The results of the multivariate analysis are reported first without the inclusion of the control variables and then with the control variables included. The results are interpreted and discussed and a summation of the findings is then presented. The relationship between the dependency indicators and the growth of inequality is not investigated due to insufficient data.

Data Analysis: Inequality

Table 7.1 presents the descriptive statistics for the dependent variable inequality. Data on inequality from the World Bank for LDCs are much less complete than the data for GNP per capita growth. Consequently, the number of valid cases is significantly reduced and the probability of achieving statistically significant findings is also reduced. Furthermore, no data at all are available on inequality for a large number of countries in the sample. Thus, for inequality, the number of valid cases is reduced to only 183.

Table 7.1: Inequality Statistics

Valid Cases	183
Mean	14.25
Variance	88.82
Standard Deviation	9.42
Minimum	2.83
Maximum	62.3

The indicator used to tap inequality is the wealth held by the wealthiest 20 percent of the population in proportion to the wealth held by the poorest 20 percent. Using this indicator, the higher the indicator, the higher the inequality. Inequality in LDCs, as these figures in Table 7.1 testify, has indeed been quite high by developed world standards. In states designated by the World Bank as "high income" over the same time period, the average inequality measure is 6.43; hence, inequality in LDCs was more than double that of high income countries during the time period of analysis. The range is also quite large from the 2.83 for Sri Lanka in 1992 to the 62.3 for Zimbabwe in 1992. This figure means that the wealthiest 20 percent in Zimbabwe in 1992 possessed 62.3 times the wealth of the poorest 20 percent. These figures are staggering, but the mean of 14.25 is also high by developed world standards. If dependency can explain a large percentage of the variance and a negative relationship between dependency and inequality is observed, then the associated dependent development thesis may be supported. Table 7.2 below presents the results of the pooled regression between dependency and inequality without the inclusion of the control variables.

Pooled Regression: Inequality

Central to the thesis of Cardoso and Faletto (1979) is the contention that dependency exacerbates inequalities within LDCs. Consequently, failure to find statistically significant relationships between the dependency indicators and inequality is unsupportive of the dependency perspective.

The results from the multivariate analysis of inequality without the control variables are similar in a number of ways to the results of the analysis of the relationship between the dependency indicators and growth without controls. First, the results are generally unsupportive of the dependency perspective since seven of the eight dependency indicators fail to achieve statistical significance. Furthermore, over 98 percent of the variance in inequality remained unexplained by the dependency variables in the multivariate analysis. Additionally, the only dependency indicator that does prove to be statistically significant is the primary export variable that is positively associated with inequality consistent with dependency expectations. It should be noted that the primary export variable was also the only statistically significant dependency indicator in the bivariate analysis. The multivariate analysis shows that the relationship remains statistically significant even when all of the other dependency indicators are held constant.

Table 7.2: Dependency and Inequality: No controls

Variable	B	Standard Error	t	sig. .05	Expected by dependency	Expected by hypothesis 2
Constant	9.3567	0.9729	9.6171	yes		
Core Trade	-0.0002	0.0097	-0.0209	no	Unexpected	Expected
Trade Con.	0.0554	0.1960	0.2825	no	Unexpected	Expected
Debt Dep.	0.0081	0.0044	1.8331	no	Unexpected	Expected
Aid %GNP	-0.0509	0.0294	-1.7329	no	Unexpected	Expected
DFI%GNP	-0.0018	0.0056	-0.3272	no	Unexpected	Expected
Patents	0.0004	0.0002	1.8929	no	Unexpected	Expected
Engy. Dep.	0.0022	0.0090	0.2456	no	Unexpected	Expected
Prim. Exp.	**0.0275**	**0.0101**	**2.7153**	**yes**	**Expected**	**Unexpected**

Adjusted R2=.01 Pooled Durbin-Watson D: .64

It remains possible, however, that when the control variables are utilized, this association may not remain statistically significant. In contrast to the analysis of economic growth, however, the autocorrelation problem which was present in the analysis of GNP per capita growth is not present in the analysis of inequality as indicated by the Durbin-Watson D statistic of .64, which is within the acceptable range.

In general, the multivariate analysis between dependency and inequality without controls, like the analysis of economic growth without controls, produces results which are supportive of hypothesis #2 and unsupportive of the dependency perspective. These findings are consistent with the findings of Kohli et al. (1986) who found no relationship between MNC penetration and inequality in longitudinal analysis. Inequality is undoubtedly influenced by a number of factors, most of which do not appear to be captured by the dependency perspective. One can only speculate as to what factors may best explain inequality; however, investigations of governmental policies and cultural and historical factors would seem to be reasonable areas to investigate in the future.

Nevertheless, the relationship between the dependency indicators and inequality shall now be investigated in multivariate analysis with the control variables implemented in order to determine if the observed relationship between primary exports and inequality remains statistically significant when the control variables are held constant. It is also possible that other dependency indicators could prove to be significant when proper controls are included. The results of the pooled regression involving dependency and inequality with the control variables are presented below in Table 7.3.

Pooled Regression: Inequality With Controls

Similar to the results between dependency and growth without controls, the results of pooled regressions between dependency and inequality with the control variables produce a very low R2 and leave over 95 percent of the variance unexplained. Additionally, seven of the eight dependency indicators fail to achieve statistical significance. As previously discussed, the low observed R2 and lack of statistical significance is unsupportive of the "new dependency" position of Cardoso (1973) and Cardoso and Faletto (1979) that dependency produces inequality.

A number of observations can be drawn from the fact that so little of the variance in inequality is explained in the multivariate analysis. First, the results infer that factors other than dependency may be more important than dependency in explaining income inequality within LDCs. Second, since control variables are included in the analysis with the result that 95 percent of the variance remains unexplained, the control variables regime type, GNP, economic growth, area, and population growth are also of limited utility for explaining inequality. Instead, explanation of the variance in inequality in LDCs may require analysis of state-political-economic policies, cultural factors, and historical factors which may be more plausible areas of investigation for explaining inequalities than dependency.

Table 7.3: Dependency and Inequality with Controls

Variable	B	Standard Error	t	sig. .05	Expected by dependency	Expected by hypothesis 2
Constant	7.0537	1.2815	5.5044	yes		
Core Trade	0.0068	0.0097	0.7010	no	Unexpected	Expected
Trade Con.	0.1901	0.1961	0.9693	no	Unexpected	Expected
Debt Dep	0.0068	0.0044	1.5581	no	Unexpected	Expected
Aid %GNP	-0.0484	0.0293	-1.6545	no	Unexpected	Expected
DFI%GNP	-0.0021	0.0055	-0.3799	no	Unexpected	Expected
Patents	0.0002	0.0003	0.7517	no	Unexpected	Expected
Energy Dep.	0.0022	0.0089	0.2526	no	Unexpected	Expected
Primary Ex.	**0.0297**	**0.0108**	**2.7479**	**yes**	**Expected**	**Unexpected**
GNP	-0.0000	0.0000	-0.1040	no	Expected	Unexpected
Pop Growth	0.2910	0.2465	1.1805	no	Expected	Unexpected
Area	**0.0000**	**0.0000**	**3.5573**	**yes**	**Expected**	**Unexpected**
GNP per Ca.	0.0003	0.0002	1.0781	no	Expected	Unexpected
Regime	0.2586	0.7121	0.3632	no	Unexpected	Unexpected
Growth	-0.0317	0.0253	-1.2534	no	Unexpected	Unexpected

Adjusted R2=.05 Pooled Durbin-Watson D: .65

Despite the small R2 in the multivariate analysis, there are a number of important results which merit discussion. Among the most important findings are the results of the direct foreign investment variable since previous empirical studies (Bornschier 1978; Bornschier and Ballmer Cao, 1979) found stocks of direct foreign investment (DFI) to be positively linked to inequality. These scholars differentiate between stocks and flows of DFI which were used here; however, they acknowledge that after a period of time flows become stocks. Since the time period of analysis in this study is 26 years, one would expect little difference in impact between stocks and flows. Unlike the findings of these previous scholars, however, no statistically significant relationship is found between direct foreign investment and inequality in the multivariate analysis. The discrepancies between these results and the ones achieved by previous scholars may be due to their use of stocks of foreign investment for only one year (1965) in the previous studies versus the longitudinal data employed here. The results here are, instead, consistent with the findings of Kohli et al. (1986) who found no statistically significant relationship between inequality and penetration by multinational corporations in their longitudinal analysis.

In contrast to the multivariate analysis of economic growth, the statistically significant positive relationship between primary exports and the dependent variable inequality does not disappear when the control variables are included in the analysis. Furthermore, the Durbin-Watson D-statistic of .65 is once again within the acceptable range, suggesting that problems of autocorrelation have not undermined the reliability of the t-statistics. Hence, the dependency position that reliance on raw material exports contributes to social inequities is supported.

The impact of the primary exports variable on inequality, however, appears to be marginal. The B coefficient for nonfuel primary products as a percentage of total exports was a very low 0.0297. This indicates that a 1 percent increase in nonfuel raw material exports as a percentage of total exports is associated only with a 0.0297 increase in the proportion of wealth owned by the wealthiest twenty percent to the proportion of wealth owned by the poorest 20 percent within LDCs. Given this low B coefficient and the low R2, one is forced to conclude that reliance on primary exports, like the other dependency indicators, is of very limited utility for explaining dependency.

In addition to the lack of explanatory power of the dependency indicators, the results also suggest that the control variables may be equally unimportant in explaining inequality. The only control variable which achieves statistical significance is area which produces a B coefficient of zero, suggesting that it essentially has no relationship with inequality when all of the other factors are held constant.

Of particular importance, however, is the regime variable which dependency theorists (O'Donnell, 1973) expect to be negatively associated with inequality. The basic argument of O'Donnell is that authoritarian regimes are necessary in dependent LDCs in order to control the masses who will be discontent due to the inequality produced by the dependent economy. No support is observed for this argument in the analysis here since the regime variable failed to achieve statistical significance.

Similarly, support for the dependency perspective failed to materialize in the relationship between GNP per capita growth and inequality. Cardoso and Faletto (1979) argue that the kind of growth which occurs in LDCs produces inequalities; hence, new dependency theorists would expect a positive relationship between GNP per capita growth and inequality. GNP per capita growth did not, however, prove to be statistically significant. This finding, along with the statistical insignificance of the vast majority of the dependency indicators, again poses a number of difficult questions for the dependency perspective. Essentially, why do these dependency indicators not explain a larger portion of the variance in inequality and why do growth and regime type fail to produce statistically significant associations with inequality? Granted, dependency theorists may argue that the statistical insignificance of the dependency indicators is a data problem related to the low (183) number of cases. Unfortunately, resolution of this problem can only be achieved in the future when more inequality data becomes available on LDCs.

At present, one can only conclude from the data analysis that very little support is found for the dependency positions on inequality, and the findings are generally consistent with hypothesis #2 that dependency is unrelated to inequality. In sum, over 95 percent of the variance in inequality remains unexplained by the dependency indicators and the control variables and only one dependency variable (primary exports) exhibits a relationship consistent with the dependency perspective, albeit the observed relationship is weak. Results regarding the important control variables regime type and GNP per capita growth are also statistically insignificant. Hence, the dependency perspective receives little support from the analysis of the dependency-inequality relationship.

Dependency and Growth of Inequality

Admittedly, though dependency appears to have little or no importance for understanding inequality, it remains possible that it may be useful as a concept which explains the growth in inequality. Unfortunately, this possibility cannot be investigated here because data on inequality are simply too sparse to engage in meaningful analysis. Thus, the question of whether dependency contributes to greater or lesser inequality must remain at present unsolved due to lack of sufficient data. There is, however, hope for the future as data gathering becomes more abundant and precise throughout the Third World. Investigation of the relationship between dependency and the growth of inequality may be possible in the future.

Chapter 8

Dependency and PQLI

The relationship between the dependency indicators and PQLI and PQLI growth (hereafter, Quality Improvement) are investigated in the following sections through the employment of multivariate analysis. First, descriptive statistics for PQLI are presented followed by the presentation of the results of the pooled regressions involving PQLI. The dependency indicators are first regressed on PQLI without the control variables, and then with the control variables in a manner consistent with the previous investigation of the dependent variables wealth, growth, and inequality. Similar analyses are then conducted on the Quality Improvement dependent variable. A summation of the findings is then presented.

Data Analysis: PQLI

Despite the weakness of the dependency indicators in explaining wealth, growth, and inequality, dependency arguments may yet prove to have much relevance if the independent variables are useful in explaining PQLI. Dependency theorists (Cardoso, 1973; Cardoso and Faletto, 1979) argue that associated-dependent development tends to have deleterious effects on quality of life within LDCs. Hence, if the dependency indicators exhibit a negative relationship with PQLI, then this aspect of new dependency theory is supported.

PQLI is a composite index of literacy, infant mortality, and life expectancy calculated from World Bank data over the 26 year time period under analysis for the 77 countries included in the sample. Data on literacy are somewhat sparse; therefore, the number of cases for analysis reduced from the possible 462 to 372. The descriptive statistics for PQLI are presented in Table 8.1 below.

Table 8.1: Physical Quality of Life Index

Valid Cases	372
Mean	57.011
Variance	507.9742
Standard Deviation	22.53
Minimum	9.6
Maximum	97.63

The possible range of PQLI is from 0 to 100. A score of 0 would mean that a country scored the lowest of all of the countries in the sample on all three PQLI components: literacy, infant mortality rates, and life expectancy. A score

of 100 means that a country scored the highest of all countries on all three of the
PQLI indicators. The mean for PQLI (57.01) is quite low by developed world
standards. In comparison, PQLI for high income states over the same period
averages 97.35. Similar to the other independent variables, PQLI exhibited a
wide range from the 9.6 for Sierra Leone in 1967 to the 97.63 for Jamaica in
1992. With such a wide range in PQLI among LDCs, if dependency is a major
factor in explaining the variance, then dependency may prove to be a useful
concept.

Pooled Regression: PQLI

First, the relationship between the dependency indicators and PQLI is
analyzed without the inclusion of the control variables. The analysis reveals how
much of the variance in PQLI the dependency indicators account for by
themselves, and the impact of each of the dependency variables when all of the
others are held constant can be assessed. The results of the data analysis
investigating this relationship are presented below in Table 8.2.

Table 8.2: Dependency and PQLI: No controls

Variable	B	Standard Error	t	sig. .05	Expected by dependency	Expected by hypothesis 3
Constant	59.1940	3.9539	14.971	yes		
Core Trade	0.0184	0.0379	0.4856	no	Unexpected	Unexpected
Trade Con.	**-1.9303**	**0.7742**	**-2.4935**	**yes**	**Expected**	**Unexpected**
Debt Dep.	**0.0643**	**0.0172**	**3.7347**	**yes**	**Unexpected**	**Expected**
Aid %GNP	**-0.3698**	**0.1150**	**-3.2158**	**yes**	**Expected**	**Unexpected**
DFI%GNP	-0.0023	0.0220	-0.1035	no	Unexpected	Unexpected
Tech. Indep.	0.0002	0.0009	0.2651	no	Unexpected	Unexpected
Energy. Ind.	-0.0628	0.0351	-1.7869	no	Unexpected	Unexpected
Primary Ex.	**-0.1848**	**0.0400**	**-4.6153**	**yes**	**Expected**	**Unexpected**

Adjusted R2=.11   Pooled Durbin-Watson D: .717

The relationship between dependency and PQLI does not appear to be
strong. Over 89 percent of the variance in PQLI remains unexplained by the
dependency variables and four of the eight variables did not prove to be
statistically significant at the .05 level. Despite these weaknesses, there is some
evidence in the results which is supportive of dependency theory. Trade partner
concentration, reliance on nonfuel primary products in exports, and aid as a
percentage of GNP all produced statistically significant figures in the direction
predicted by dependency theory. Of the four statistically significant indicators,
only debt as a percentage of GNP produced a relationship with PQLI in the
direction that would not be predicted by dependency theory. The debt variable

was not statistically significant in the bivariate analysis and only becomes statistically significant when the other dependency indicators are held constant; however the B coefficient was a relatively low .0643. Essentially this suggests that an increase in debt of 1 percent of GNP is associated with only a .06 positive unit change in PQLI. In other words, though the positive association between debt and PQLI is inconsistent with dependency theory, its impact appears to be marginal.

In bivariate analysis, aid was observed to have the strongest negative association with PQLI of all of the dependency indicators. When all of the other dependency indicators are held constant, this relationship remains strong. The B coefficient reveals that an increase in aid of 1 percent of GNP is associated with approximately a .37 unit decrease in PQLI when all of the other dependency indicators are held constant. This finding is consistent with the dependency perspective and at least leaves open the possibility that aid is being misdirected, and therefore, fails to positively affect the elements which compose PQLI; however, it remains possible that this relationship will disappear when controls are included in the analysis.

Trade partner concentration was also statistically significant in bivariate analysis, exhibiting a positive .12 association with PQLI. When all of the dependency indicators are held constant, trade concentration remains statistically significant, but the direction of the relationship between trade concentration and PQLI changes to negative. This change in sign suggests that the results achieved in bivariate analysis are spurious, and that the other dependency variables tend to confound the relationship between trade concentration and PQLI. Additionally, the B coefficient of -1.93 appears quite large, suggesting that trade concentration may have serious negative effects on PQLI in a manner consistent with the dependency perspective. It remains possible, however, that this relationship will disappear when the control variables are implemented in the analysis.

Primary exports are also observed to have a statistically significant negative relationship with PQLI in bivariate analysis. When all of the other dependency indicators are held constant in multivariate analysis, the relationship remains negative and statistically significant, consistent with dependency arguments. The B coefficient for primary exports reveals that it may be less important than aid and trade partner concentration in explaining PQLI; however, the findings suggest that the "unequal exchange" relationship which is so vital to the dependency perspective is also important in explaining PQLI. Once again, further analysis is needed in order to determine if the primary exports variable remains consistent with dependency theory when proper controls are implemented.

In sum, though some support for dependency theory was observed in the multivariate analysis, it must be reiterated that the dependency indicators only explained 11 percent of the variance in PQLI; hence, a great number of other factors may be more important in explaining PQLI than dependency. It is also possible that these findings are spurious and that the negative relationship of dependency indicators with PQLI is merely a function of other factors such as small geographic area, low per capita GNP, rapid population growth, or rapid GNP growth. Hence, these controls will be implemented in order to determine the nature of the dependency/PQLI relationships when these other factors are held constant. Below in Table 8.3 are the results of the pooled regression involving dependency and PQLI with control variables included.

Pooled Regression with Controls: PQLI

The pooled regression involving PQLI and dependency with the control variables explained over twice as much of the variance (.28) as the dependency indicators explained without controls (.11). These results suggest that the control variables may be more important factors for explaining PQLI than the dependency indicators. This finding is in contradiction with the consensus of dependency theorists (Chilcote and Edelstein, 1974) that the prosperity of a dependent economy is primarily a function of international economic events.

Importantly, the previously observed relationship between primary exports and PQLI failed to achieve statistical significance when the control variables were added. This finding is particularly damaging to the "unequal exchange" thesis of the dependency perspective, another consensus of dependency scholars according to Chilcote and Edelstein (1974). In essence, even if reliance on primary exports is a mechanism for transferring economic surplus to the core at the expense of the periphery, it does not have negative effects on PQLI.

Perhaps the best support for dependency is in the relationship between trade concentration and PQLI. The observed negative relationship between the two variables is consistent with the arguments of Frank (1967) that trade ties with the core have negative effects on development in the periphery. Additionally, the behavior of the trade partner concentration variable is at odds with the stated hypothesis #3. The B coefficient for trade partner concentration reveals that a one percent increase in trade with the top two core trading partners as a percentage of total trade is associated with a decrease in PQLI of 1.52 units. The findings obviously have policy implications in that trade diversification may be a policy course for states seeking to improve PQLI. This strong negative relationship between trade concentration and PQLI is less important, however, if trade concentration is not negatively associated with Quality Improvement. If improvement of PQLI is the goal, then it is necessary to investigate what factors may be associated with Quality Improvement. Multivariate analysis of Quality Improvement is, therefore, needed to gain a better understanding of the importance of trade concentration and the other dependency indicators on development.

Aid as a percentage of GNP, like trade concentration, is observed to have a statistically significant negative relationship with PQLI when all of the other variables are held constant. Furthermore, the relationship appears strong. The B coefficient for aid reveals that a one percent increase in aid as a percentage of GNP is associated with a .286 decrease in PQLI. This finding is consistent with the consensus of the dependency perspective (Chilcote and Edelstein, 1974); that the responsiveness of dependent economies to external factors yield benefits only for the upper classes and none for the masses.

Table 8.3: Dependency and PQLI With Controls

Variable	B	Standard Error	t	sig. .05	Expected by dependency	Expected by hypoth. 3
Constant	51.2002	4.7816	10.708	yes		
Core Trade	-0.0169	0.0352	-0.4813	no	Unexpected	Unexpected
Trade Con.	**-1.5283**	**0.7116**	**-2.1476**	**yes**	**Expected**	**Unexpected**
Debt %GNP	**0.0606**	**0.0160**	**3.8015**	**yes**	**Unexpected**	**Expected**
Aid %GNP	**-0.2862**	**0.1067**	**-2.6821**	**yes**	**Expected**	**Unexpected**
DFI%GNP	-0.0008	0.0200	-0.0406	no	Unexpected	Unexpected
Patents	-0.0011	0.0009	-1.1930	no	Unexpected	Unexpected
Energy Dep.	-0.0468	0.0323	-1.4491	no	Unexpected	Unexpected
Primary Ex.	-0.0600	0.0395	-1.5180	no	Unexpected	Unexpected
GNP	**0.0001**	**0.0000**	**2.1754**	**yes**	**Unexpected**	**Expected**
Pop Growth	**-3.7277**	**0.8942**	**-4.1687**	**yes**	**Unexpected**	**Expected**
Area	-0.0000	0.0000	-1.3207	no	Expected	Unexpected
GNP per ca.	**0.0040**	**0.0008**	**4.7146**	**yes**	**Unexpected**	**Expected**
Regime	**10.5188**	**2.5859**	**4.0678**	**yes**	**Expected**	**Expected**
Inequality	**0.4546**	**0.1715**	**2.6514**	**yes**	**Unexpected**	**Expected**
Growth	0.0500	0.0923	0.5418	no	Unexpected	Unexpected

Adjusted R2=.28   Pooled Durbin-Watson D: .81

Contrary to the relationships observed between aid and trade partner concentration, debt as a percentage of GNP proved to display a positive association with PQLI. Consequently, the statistically significant dependency variables proved to exhibit a mixed relationship with PQLI with two variables negatively (trade concentration and aid) associated with PQLI and one (debt) positive, contrary to the expectations of both the dependency perspective and hypothesis #3. The positive relationship between debt as a percentage of GNP and PQLI may infer that a portion of capital borrowed by LDCs is redistributed in such a way that it has a positive impact on literacy, life expectancy, and infant mortality rates. This finding is contrary to a consensus of dependency scholars (Chilcote and Edelstein, 1974) who contend that borrowing in the periphery benefits only national and international elites. Conversely, the finding is consistent with hypothesis #3 that greater dependency (in this case in the form of debt) is associated with increased PQLI. Debt, however, appears to have less impact on the dependent variable than trade concentration and aid, as indicated by the lower B coefficient. The B coefficient for debt reveals that every one percent increase in debt as a percentage of GNP, was associated with a .06 increase in PQLI. Consequently, debt does not appear to have a strong association with PQLI since an increase in debt as a percentage of GNP from 0 to 100 percent is associated with a PQLI increase of only six. Therefore, though the findings are inconsistent with the dependency perspective, they are only mildly supportive of hypothesis #3.

In addition to the statistical significance of the three dependency variables, the five control variables, GNP per capita, GNP, population growth, inequality, and regime type all achieved statistical significance at the .05 level. The fact that these variables proved to be significant at all tends to undermine the dependency perspective since the dependency perspective allows little room for the impact of internal forces on development (Chilcote and Edelstein, 1974).

It is not surprising that GNP per capita is associated with PQLI; however, the observation is damaging to dependency theory since it suggests that the lower classes do receive some benefits as wealth increases in LDCs. The B coefficient for GNP per capita reveals that a $1,000 increase in GNP per capita is associated with a four unit increase in PQLI. Obviously, the association between GNP per capita and PQLI appears to be very strong. This finding is contradictory with the dependency consensus (Chilcote and Edelstein, 1974) that the masses receive no benefits from dependent development.

Population growth also exhibited a relationship with PQLI which appears to be contradictory with the dependency perspective and in congruence with liberal modernization perspectives. The B coefficients reveal that a one percent increase in population growth is associated with a decrease in PQLI of 3.73. Clearly, low PQLI is associated with high population growth. This finding is unsupportive of the dependency consensus (Chilcote and Edelstein, 1974) that development is primarily a function of international economic events since population growth is essentially an internal variable.

The statistically significant positive relationship between inequality and PQLI also seriously undermines the dependency perspective. The B coefficient for inequality reveals that a one percent increase in the proportion of the wealth owned by the wealthiest twenty percent to that of the lowest twenty percent is associated with a .455 increase in PQLI.   The basic argument of new dependency theorists (Cardoso and Faletto, 1979) that inequality has deleterious effects on the lower classes is unsupported. This finding is instead congruent with the liberal perspective under which all classes benefit from economic development, including the lower classes (Snider, 1971, p. 426). The covariance of inequality and PQLI under the liberal perspective is then explained through the prosperity of the upper classes in comparison to the lower classes, rather than at the expense of the lower classes.

Democratic regime types also have a strong positive association with PQLI. The B coefficient for regime type reveals that the presence of a democratic regime is associated with a PQLI which is over 10 points higher than those of nondemocratic regimes when the other variables are held constant. Although new dependency theorists, such as O'Donnell (1979) and Cardoso (1973), infer that democratic regimes are desirable for the benefit of the lower classes, radical dependency theorists such as Frank (1967) eschew democracy in favor of socialist revolution. Hence, depending on the segment of dependency theory to which one subscribes, the findings may or may not be congruent with the dependency perspective. The results are certainly supportive of the modernization arguments of Lipset (1963, p. 31).

One other control variable, GNP, also achieved statistical significance, but does not appear to be substantively significant. The very low B coefficient of 0.0001 reveals that there is virtually no association between GNP and PQLI. In a similar vein, area and GNP per capita growth failed to achieve statistical significance in the pooled regression. Consequently, the contention of dependency theorists (Cardoso, 1973; Cardoso, and Faletto, 1979) that dependent growth produces deleterious effects on the lower classes is unsupported.

In sum, only three of eight dependency variables were observed to be statistically significant in their relationship with PQLI. Any deleterious effects of the positive relationship between direct foreign investment and inequality observed by Bornschier et al. (1978) are somewhat undermined by the observation that direct foreign investment is unrelated to PQLI. This finding along with the statistical insignificance of the majority of the dependency indicators again poses several difficult questions for the dependency perspective. The results show that the dependency indicators are of limited use for explaining PQLI in LDCs. Dependency and the control variables did account for over one fourth of the variance in PQLI; however, the dependency indicators without controls explained barely over ten percent. Furthermore, debt and inequality were observed to have statistically significant positive relationships with PQLI, which are difficult to explain through dependency theory. In this respect, the findings are unsupportive of the dependency perspective; however, hypothesis #3, that dependency is positively related to PQLI, is also unsupported. Instead, the position that is best supported from the results is that dependency is unrelated to PQLI.

Data Analysis: Quality Improvement

Quality Improvement represents a percentage calculated by dividing the difference in PQLI for any two consecutive five year time points, for example, 1992 and 1987, by the PQLI of the earlier of the two time points. Since data for PQLI are unavailable prior to 1967, the growth periods that are analyzed are 1967-72, 1973-77, 1978-82, 1983-87, and 1988-92. Growth rates are calculated over five year intervals instead of annually, due to the sparse nature of the data. With only five time periods of growth, the data for the independent variables for 1967 were coded as missing to produce the five time points of dependency which coincide with the growth years. Hence, the analysis essentially will determine if dependency in 1972 is associated with the Quality Improvement from 1968-1972 and if dependency in 1977 is associated with Quality Improvement from 1973-77 etc. The omission of 77 cases due to insufficient data on PQLI from the 1960's reduces the data set to 324 valid cases. The descriptive statistics for Quality Improvement are presented in Table 8.4 .

Table 8.4: Quality Improvement Statistics

Valid Cases	324
Mean	11.96
Variance	148.94
Standard Deviation	12.20
Minimum	-20.9
Maximum	84.75

Perhaps the most striking result from the descriptive statistics presented in table 8.4 is that the average Quality Improvement over a five-year period was 11.96 percent. In other words, the physical quality of life index increased an average of 11.96 percent in LDCs during each five-year period despite the conditions of dependency that are hypothesized to have existed. This finding, in and of itself, presents difficulties for dependency theory since consensus of the dependency perspective (Chilcote and Edelstein, 1974) is that only the upper classes benefit from dependent development. Widespread Quality Improvement suggests that the lower classes may receive some benefits of dependent economic growth. This finding does not, however, mean that dependency is positively associated with Quality Improvement, only that Quality Improvement did rise on the average within LDCs. Multivariate analysis is needed to determine if the greatest Quality Improvement is associated with either greater or lesser dependency among LDCs. The results of the pooled regressions involving the eight dependency indicators and Quality Improvement without the inclusion of the control variables are presented in Table 8.5 below.

Pooled Regression: Quality Improvement

The dependency indicators themselves without control variables appear to be of little utility for explaining Quality Improvement. Over 97 percent of the variance remains unexplained by the dependency variables and only one variable, aid, proved to be statistically significant exhibiting a positive association with Improvement. This finding on aid is contrary to the dependency consensus (Chilcote and Edelstein, 1974) that only the upper classes within LDCs benefit from contact with the core. The B coefficient for the aid variable reveals that a one percent increase in aid as a percentage of GNP is associated with an Improvement rate which is higher by .1865. These results not only suggest that aid is an important factor in increasing improvement, but are consistent with the liberal perspectives of Cline (1975) and Ellsworth (1969) who argue that aid works to equalize income, and therefore, benefits the lower as well as the upper classes.

In general, however, since aid is the only statistically significant variable and only 3 percent of the variance is explained, the analysis is unsupportive of Hypothesis #3. Instead of dependency fostering Quality Improvement, it appears to be for the most part unrelated to Quality Improvement. This includes the associations between Improvement and trade concentration and energy independence, which produced statistically significant results that were consistent with dependency expectations in the bivariate analysis, but disappeared in multivariate analysis.

Table 8.5: Dependency and Quality Improvement: No controls.

Variable	B	Standard Error	t	sig. .05	Expected by dependency	Expected by hypothesis 3
Constant	9.8879	1.5140	6.5312	yes		
Core Trade	-0.0290	0.0196	-1.4821	no	Unexpected	Unexpected
Trade Con.	0.1762	0.3441	0.5121	no	Unexpected	Unexpected
Debt %GNP	-0.0019	0.0090	-0.2152	no	Unexpected	Unexpected
Aid %GNP	**0.1865**	**0.0605**	**3.0835**	**yes**	**Unexpected**	**Expected**
DFI%GNP	0.0069	0.0102	0.6742	no	Unexpected	Unexpected
Patents	-0.0005	0.0005	-1.0920	no	Unexpected	Unexpected
Energy Dep.	0.0135	0.0190	0.7110	no	Unexpected	Unexpected
Primary Ex.	0.0142	0.0175	0.8113	no	Unexpected	Unexpected

Adjusted R2=.03   Pooled Durbin-Watson D: 1.61

Similarly, the observed negative relationship between trade partner concentration and PQLI is not detected in the analysis of Quality Improvement. Dependency theorists would predict, however, that the impact of aid on Quality Improvement would be confounded by other factors such as regime type and inequality. The arguments that the utility of aid in increasing PQLI may be reduced under authoritarian regimes or in states with relatively large income gaps are certainly plausible; therefore, controls should be included for these factors. Certainly, GNP per capita growth may also play a role if there is a growth-equity trade-off or if rapid growth tends to create "discontinuities" and extremist politics as Lipset (1963, p. 54) argues. GNP, GNP per capita, population growth, and area are also included as controls in the analysis reported below in Table 8.6

Pooled Regression: Quality Improvement with Controls

The results of the pooled regression involving Quality Improvement and dependency and the control variables proved to be similar to the results of multivariate analysis of Quality Improvement without controls. The results are generally unsupportive of dependency theory, but almost equally unsupportive of Hypothesis #3. The adjusted R2 of 0.03 and the statistical insignificance of seven of eight dependency indicators suggest that dependency is an almost meaningless concept for explaining the variance in Quality Improvement. Since dependency appears to have little or no value for understanding Quality Improvement, support is not observed for the arguments of Cardoso (1973, p. 9) that dependent development is a skewed development which tends to "create a restricted, limited and upper class oriented type of market and society" which is "contradictory, and exploitive" of the masses in society.

Additionally, The negative relationship between trade concentration and PQLI which emerges from the analysis of PQLI does not resurface in the analysis of Quality Improvement since trade concentration fails to achieve statistical significance in the analysis; hence, the argument that trade concentration has deleterious effects on PQLI is weakened.

Similarly, unsupported again is the dependency inference of Cardoso (1973) that dependency produces inequality which, in turn, has deleterious effects of the quality of life of the lower classes. The inequality variable failed to achieve statistical significance; hence, we are without evidence that inequality itself is a hindrance to Quality Improvement. Similarly, the regime variable failed to produce statistical significance in its association with Quality Improvement; therefore, even if dependency does produce authoritarianism as claimed by O'Donnell (1973) and Cardoso (1973), evidence is not observed which suggests that authoritarian regimes experience lower rates of Quality Improvement than democratic regimes.

Table 8.6: Dependency and Quality Improvement With Controls

Variable	B	Standard Error	t	sig. .05	Expected by dependency	Expected by hypothesis 3
Constant	12.0594	2.4223	4.9785	yes		
Core Trade	-0.0274	0.0202	-1.3578	no	Unexpected	Unexpected
Trade Con.	0.1533	0.3480	0.4406	no	Unexpected	Unexpected
Debt %GNP	0.0023	0.0094	0.2426	no	Unexpected	Unexpected
Aid %GNP	**0.1531**	**0.0627**	**2.4409**	**yes**	**Unexpected**	**Expected**
DFI%GNP	0.0063	0.0101	0.6218	no	Unexpected	Unexpected
Patents	-0.0004	0.0005	-0.8383	no	Unexpected	Unexpected
Energy Dep.	0.0056	0.0191	0.2916	no	Unexpected	Unexpected
Primary Ex.	0.0023	0.0196	0.1196	no	Unexpected	Unexpected
GNP	-0.0000	0.0000	-0.3238	no	Expected	Unexpected
Pop Growth	0.2471	0.4136	0.5975	no	Expected	Unexpected
Area	0.0000	0.0000	0.4699	no	Expected	Unexpected
GNP per ca.	-0.0001	0.0004	-0.1338	no	Expected	Unexpected
Regime	-1.3534	1.4084	-0.9610	no	Unexpected	Unexpected
Inequality	-0.0428	0.0232	-1.8414	no	Unexpected	Expected
Growth	0.0118	0.0641	-0.9610	no	Unexpected	Expected

Adjusted R2=0.03   Pooled Durbin-Watson D: 1.67

Also failing to achieve statistical significance is the relationship between GNP per capita growth and Quality Improvement. Cardoso (1973) argues that the type of growth present in dependent economies is a distorted growth which benefits only the upper classes at the expense of the lower; therefore, one should expect dependent growth to be accompanied by slower rates of Quality

Improvement (which represents a betterment of conditions throughout the entire society). No evidence of such a negative relationship between Quality Improvement and GNP per capita growth is observed; consequently, the dependency perspective is unsupported. It should be noted, however, that the liberal modernization paradigm, which would expect all segments of society to benefit from GNP per capita growth, and therefore, posit a positive relationship between GNP per capita growth and Quality Improvement, is also unsupported by the results. The results suggest that Quality Improvement is best explained by factors other than GNP per capita growth. Perhaps government policies are viable alternative areas which may better explain Quality Improvement.

The remaining control variables, population growth, area, GNP, and GNP per capita, are observed to be statistically insignificant. The results for population growth are particularly important since population growth is negatively associated with PQLI. The results reveal that, despite this negative association with PQLI, no evidence is observed which suggests that population growth impedes Quality Improvement. GNP per capita was observed to be negatively associated with Quality Improvement in bivariate analysis; however, that relationship disappears when controls are implemented in multivariate analysis.

In sum, dependency appears to have little utility for explaining Quality Improvement with some 97 percent of the variance unexplained by dependency and the control variables. No dependency indicator exhibited an association with Quality Improvement which proved to be consistent with dependency theory. Only one dependency indicator, aid, achieves statistical significance in its association with Quality Improvement. Aid, however, is positively associated with Quality Improvement contrary to dependency expectations. Also important, no statistically significant association is produced between trade concentration and Quality Improvement despite the previously observed negative association between trade concentration and PQLI. Additionally, no relationship is observed between Quality Improvement and the control variables, GNP per capita growth, regime type, and inequality. Since these variables are expected to be negatively associated with Quality Improvement by dependency scholars (Cardoso, 1973), these results are also unsupportive of the dependency perspective.

The only manner in which the relationships proved to be consistent with the dependency perspective was in the statistical insignificance of the control variables, GNP, GNP per capita, population growth, and area. Though these observations are consistent with dependency expectations since dependency allows little room for such internal factors in explaining the condition of the lower classes, they are not the focus of dependency theory.

Conversely, the findings provide weak support for Hypothesis #3, with only aid exhibiting a relationship supportive of the hypothesis. The positive relationship between aid and Improvement undermines dependency arguments which could be built on the previously observed negative relationship between aid and PQLI. The results regarding the aid variable are of additional value since they have important policy implications. Essentially, the results suggest that increases in foreign aid are a viable strategy for LDCs which have Quality Improvement as a goal. Furthermore, since regime type did not prove to be statistically significant, aid may be useful for stimulating Quality Improvement in authoritarian states, as well as within democracies. Hence, if the purpose of aid is to enhance the Quality Improvement in LDCs, regime type may not be the best criterion for discrimination in aid donations. In general, dependency does not appear to be a concern for policymakers in the area of Quality Improvement.

Chapter 9

Summary and Conclusions

This research is called for because of the current widespread policy directions chosen by LDCs that include marketization and integration into the capitalist world economy. The liberal marketization strategy is prevalent despite the warnings of a major social science perspective on development, the dependency perspective, that tends to view integration into the capitalist world economy as detrimental to economic and poltical development in LDCs. This research is an empirical attempt to assess the merits of this perspective.

Within this empirical study, the two alternative perspectives of economic development, namely, the liberal modernization perspective and the Marxist-oriented dependency perspective, were identified, explained, and compared. Relevant literature surrounding the dependency perspective was reviewed, including both consensus and disagreements within and without the dependency perspective. In subsequent chapters, the results of previous empirical research on dependency relationships was surveyed, culminating in the formulation of three hypotheses which are contradictory with the dependency perspective.

The hypotheses are based upon the liberal notion that core-periphery contact and capitalist economic development are beneficial for LDCs and that these benefits are not limited to the upper classes. The hypotheses that are presented can be quickly summarized as the expectation that dependency is positively related to both economic growth and improvement of PQLI and unrelated to inequality.

In order to test these hypotheses, indicators of dependency for seventy-seven nations over the time period from 1967 to 1992 are chosen based upon the empirical works of previous scholars and general contentions of dependency theorists. Control variables were selected and implemented into the analysis based upon intuition, logic, and previous literature which stressed the importance of these factors in economic development.

Factor analysis reveals that the variables chosen to indicate dependency are multidimensional in character. The majority of the relationships revealed in the bivariate analysis do not provide support for the dependency perspective; however, a minority of bivariate relationships are consistent with dependency expectations. Multivariate analysis was, therefore, employed to better understand the nature of the observed relationships.

Multivariate analysis reveals that the indicators chosen to represent dependency are of limited usefulness in explaining each of the dependent variables. Without the inclusion of the control variables, the dependency indicators did not explain over 15 percent of the variance in any of the

121

dependent variables. Interestingly, the dependency indicators exhibited the least explanatory power with the inequality variable producing an R2 of .01. This observation is consistent with Hypothesis #2 (that dependency is unrelated to inequality) and inconsistent with the arguments of Cardoso (1973) that dependency produces inequality. Support was not observed, however, for Hypotheses #1 (dependency is positively related to GNP per capita growth in LDCs) and since the small percentage of the variance explained in multivariate analysis suggests that dependency is of limited usefulness for explaining wealth and growth. Similarly, Hypothesis #3 (dependency is positively related to growth in physical quality of life in LDCs) is unsupported due to the small percentage of the variance explained by the dependency indicators and the failure of the dependency indicators to produce statistically significant associations in the majority of cases. Conversely, the findings regarding the dependency indicators and wealth, growth, PQLI, and Quality Improvement are equally unsupportive of the dependency perspective since the dependency indicators do not explain a large proportion of the variance in the dependent variables as dependency theory would predict.

Table 9.1 below provides a picture of the results of the bivariate and multivariate analyses and the behavior of the individual dependency indicators is summarized. The B coefficients reported in Table 9.1 are those which are produced with the control variables included in the analysis.

Despite the failure of the dependency indicators to explain much of the variance in the dependent variables, portions of dependency theory could receive significant support from the analysis if individual dependency indicators proved to exhibit relationships with the dependent variables which are consistent with dependency theory. In general, the dependency indicators do not exhibit associations with the dependent variables in the multivariate analysis that are consistent with dependency expectations; however, there are a few exceptions. The associations between the dependency indicators and the dependent variables are summarized below.

Core Trade does not exhibit associations consistent with dependency expectations since it does not produce statistically significant results either in multivariate analysis or in bivariate analysis that are consistent with dependency expectations. If there is a negative link between trade volume with the core and the dependent variables, it is not found through this empirical analysis. The only statistically significant result involving the core trade variable, a positive association between core trade and GNP per capita growth, is in the direction that is inconsistent with dependency expectations. Instead, the core trade variable is positively associated with GNP per capita growth.

Trade Partner Concentration exhibits a positive association with growth that is inconsistent with radical dependency theory, but consistent with the associated dependent development thesis (Cardoso, 1973). Also consistent with the dependency perspective, Trade Partner Concentration exhibits a negative association with PQLI in multivariate analysis; however, no statistically significant link was found in multivariate analysis between Trade Partner

Concentration and Quality Improvement. The lack of a link between Trade Partner Concentration and Quality Improvement undermines the importance of its negative association with PQLI.

Table 9.1: Composite of Analysis

Variable	Wealth	Growth	Inequality	PQLI	Improv.
Core Trade B	1.2591	**0.0440**	0.0068	-0.0169	-0.0274
Core Trade r	.23	.18	-.47	.22	-.09
Trade Concen. B	-63.003	**0.8279**	0.1901	**-1.5283**	0.1533
Trade Concen r	**-.01**	-.02	.09	**.12**	-.13
Debt %GNP B	-0.4369	**-0.0205**	0.0068	**0.0606**	0.0023
Debt % GNP r	-.10	-.19	.06	-.02	.02
Aid %GNP B	-9.0589	0.0041	-0.0484	**-0.2862**	**0.1531**
Aid %GNP r	**-.29**	-.12	.01	**-.46**	.03
DFI%GNP B	-0.4369	0.0038	-0.0021	-0.0008	0.0063
DFI%GNP r	-.02	0	-.08	-0	.03
Tech. Independence B	-0.0634	0.0003	0.0002	-0.0011	-0.0004
Tech. Independence r	**.18**	.08	.07	.25	-.14
Energy Independence B	-1.0009	0.0151	0.0022	-0.0468	0.0056
Energy Independence r	.04	.06	-.04	-.02	**.17**
Primary Export B	-9.7054	-0.0116	**0.0297**	-0.0600	0.0023
Primary Export r	**-.52**	**-.22**	**.25**	**-.35**	.15
GNP B	**0.0167**	0.0000	-0.0000	**0.0001**	-0.0000
GNP r	**.39**	.15	.04	.25	-.13
Population Growth B	78.3312	0.0621	0.2910	**-3.7277**	0.2471
Population Growth r	.05	-.02	.16	-.30	.17
Area B	**-0.0003**	**-0.0000**	**0.0000**	-0.0000	0.0000
Area r	.13	-.03	.23	.01	-.03
GNP per capita B		**0.0006**	0.0003	**0.0040**	-0.0001
GNP per capita r		**.27**	.10	**.43**	**-.19**
Inequality B				**0.4546**	-0.0428
Inequality r	.10	-.07		.10	0
GNP per cap. growth B			-0.0317	0.0500	0.0118
GNP per cap. growth r			-.07	.09	-.07
Regime Type B	**361.971**	0.2608	0.2586	**10.5188**	-1.3534
Regime Type r	**.34**	-.07	-.02	**.39**	-.18

Debt exhibits a negative association with growth consistent with dependency expectations; however, debt also exhibits a positive association with PQLI in contradiction with dependency expectations. Hence, though debt may be a hindrance to economic growth, it is not found to have adverse effects on inequality and quality of life or Quality Improvement.

Aid is observed to be negatively related to wealth in bivariate analysis, but this association disappears when controls were implemented in multivariate analysis. Consistent with dependency expectations, aid does prove to be negatively related to PQLI in both bivariate and multivariate analysis; however, aid exhibited a positive association with Quality Improvement which is inconsistent with dependency expectations. Hence, aid appears to be a viable policy alternative for improving PQLI.

Direct Foreign Investment, Technological Independence, and Energy Independence do not exhibit any statistically significant associations with the dependent variables in multivariate analysis. Consequently, no support is found for the dependency position that these variables contribute to underdevelopment and the works of previous scholars that identified links between DFI and underdevelopment are unsupported.

In contrast to these variables, the primary export variable produces bivariate associations with the dependent variables that are consistent with dependency expectations. Reliance on primary exports is negatively associated with four of the five dependent variables, Quality Improvement being the lone dependent exception. In multivariate analysis with control variables included, associations between primary exports and growth, PQLI, and Quality Improvement are not observed; however, primary exports are negatively associated with wealth and positively associated with inequality as dependency theory would predict. Hence, the best support for the dependency perspective is observed through the primary exports variable, and even in this case, the results are consistent with the dependency perspective involving only two of the five dependent variables and no statistically significant relationship involving primary exports was found involving either of the two important growth variables (GNP per capita growth, and Quality Improvement).

Also inconsistent with dependency theory is the behavior of Inequality as a control variable. Inequality is observed to be positively related to PQLI in contradiction with Cardoso's (1973, p. 176) contention that associated dependent development could lead to an increase in wealth but result in inequality which would not allow for increase in the physical quality of life.

Similarly, the results involving the regime variable are at variance with the associated dependent development thesis. No statistically significant relationship is observed between regime type and inequality. This finding is inconsistent with the theses of Cardoso (1973) and O'Donnell (1973) who link authoritarian regime type with inequality in dependent development. Instead, the only statistically significant findings involving regime type and the dependent variables are the positive associations between democratic regime types and GNP per capita and between democratic regime types and PQLI. These findings are consistent with the liberal modernization position of Lipset (1963) who views democracy and economic development as positively linked. Conversely, the findings are inconsistent with the perspective of Cardoso (1973) who argues that development is not possible in dependent economies without the installation of authoritarian regimes.

The research reported is exploratory in nature and intended to answer a number of questions concerning development. While some insight has been gained as to the relationship between dependency and economic development, the results of this research raise a number of additional questions regarding dependency and economic development, many of which remain unresolved. In general, the empirical results are unsupportive of dependency theory; however, the results are equally unsupportive of two of the three stated hypotheses. The inference to be drawn from the empirical results is that dependency is largely unrelated to economic development; however, the question which remains unanswered is that if dependency does not explain economic development, then what factors do better explain economic development?

The answers to this question are likely plural and complex in character and are unlikely to be arrived at definitively over the short term; however, the results of this research suggest that attention to external economic factors should be minimalized in favor of a strategy which focuses on internal factors such as culture and goverment policies within LDCs. It is unclear at present whether these internal factors will be of great value in explaining development; however, from the results achieved in this empirical study, it appears that dependency is not.

The policy implications of these findings are that LDCs need not abandon their liberal marketization strategies or sever their ties with the international capitalist system for fear of devolution into slow growth, inequality, authoritarianism and diminishing physical quality of life. Aid may be accepted as beneficial to Quality Improvement and trade and foreign investment need not be feared as factors which depress growth and lead to inequality. Though we cannot conclude that marketization strategies in LDCs that include greater integration into the international capitalist system will produce development in LDCs, it does not appear that these strategies will produce "underdevelopment" in the form of slower growth, greater inequality, or a lower physical quality of life.

Appendix A

The Sample

The sample of countries listed below in Figure A.1 was chosen from the World Bank's table of basic indicators and includes all non high-income countries for which there are adequate data available on all variables. The years which are included, 1967, 1972, 1977, 1982, 1987, and 1992, are chosen due to the limiting of data availability by the World Bank on quality of life indicators to these particular years only.

Algeria	Ethiopia	Morocco	Surinam
Argentina	Ghana	Nepal	Syria
Bangladesh	Guatemala	Nicaragua	Tanzania
Benin	Guinea Bissau	Niger	Thailand
Bolivia	Haiti	Nigeria	Togo
Botswana	Honduras	Oman	Trinidad/Tobago
Brazil	India	Pakistan	Tunisia
Burkina Faso	Indonesia	Panama	Uruguay
Burundi	Iran	Papua N. Guinea	Venezuela
Cameroon	Iraq	Paraguay	Zaire
Chad	Jamaica	Peru	Zambia
Chile	Kenya	Philippines	Zimbabwe
Colombia	Korea	Portugal	
Congo	Liberia	Qatar	
Costa Rica	Libya	Rwanda	
Cote d'Ivoire	Madagascar	Saudi Arabia	
Dominican Rep	Malawi	Senegal	
Ecuador	Mali	Sierra Leone	
Egypt	Malta	Somalia	
El Salvador	Mauritania	South Africa	
	Mauritius	Sri Lanka	
	Mexico	Sudan	

Appendix B

GLS Diagnostics

Below in Table B.1 are the residual variance ratios for each country involved in the analysis of dependency and GNP per capita growth. As recommended by Stimson (1985) dummy variables are added to the analysis for all states with residual variance ratios over 1.0 in an attempt to correct for autocorrelation when analyzing GNP per capita growth.

Table B.1: Residual Variance Ratios

State	Residual Var Ratio	State	Residual Var Ratio	State	Residual Var Ratio
Algeria	0.291	India	0.666	Paraguay	0.459
Argentina	0.781	Indonesia	0.450	Peru	0.333
Bangladesh	0.444	Iran	1.166	Philippines	0.179
Benin	0.510	Iraq	0.572	Portugal	**1.065**
Bolivia	**2.977**	Jamaica	0.668	Rwanda	0.343
Botswana	0.678	Kenya	**1.027**	Saudi Arabia	**2.474**
Brazil	0.509	S. Korea	**4.888**	Senegal	**3.971**
Burkina Faso	**2.271**	Liberia	**3.368**	Sierra Leone	**1.242**
Burundi	**1.308**	Libya	**2.062**	Somalia	**1.592**
Cameroon	0.618	Madagascar	**1.665**	South Africa	0.831
Chad	0.218	Malawi	0.228	Sri Lanka	0.283
Chile	0.733	Malaysia	0.261	Sudan	0.869
Colombia	0.293	Mali	**1.666**	Suriname	0.063
Congo	0.157	Malta	0.362	Syria	0.498
Costa Rica	0.453	Mauritania	0.150	Tanzania	0.856
Cote d' Ivoire	0.470	Mauritius	0.875	Thailand	0.647
Dominican R.	0.681	Mexico	0.110	Togo	0.258
Ecuador	0.317	Morocco	**1.024**	Trinidad	0.461
Egypt	0.124	Nepal	0.464	Tunisia	**5.318**
El Salvador	**1.335**	Nicaragua	0.314	Turkey	**1.458**
Ethiopia	0.786	Niger	0.663	Uruguay	0.614
Ghana	0.483	Nigeria	0.530	Venezuela	0.102
Guatemala	**1.134**	Oman	0.493	Zaire	**5.537**
Guinea Bissau	0.657	Pakistan	0.774	Zambia	**1.082**
Haiti	0.466	Panama	**2.273**	Zimbabwe	0.549
Honduras	0.930	Papua N. G.	**4.689**		

Each state highlighted in bold above is added to the analysis as a dummy variable with a one entered for that country each year and a zero code entered for all other countries. The series of dummy variables are then included in the pooled GLS ARMA analysis of the dependent variable. None of the dummy variables are statistically significant in the analysis and the inclusion of the dummy variables fails to reduce the Durbin-Watson D statistic.

Select Bibliography

Alschuler, L. R. 1976. "Satellization and Stagnation in Latin America." *International Studies Quarterly* 20: 39-83.

Almond, Gabriel. 1987. "The Development of Political Development." In Myron Weiner and Samuel Huntington eds., *Understanding Political Development*. New York: HarperCollins.

Almond, Gabriel, and Sydney Verba. 1963. *The Civic Culture*. Boston: Little, Brown.

Amin, Samir. 1974. *Accumulation on a World Scale: A Critique of the Theory of Underdevelopment*. New York: Monthly Review Press.

Anandakrishnan, M., and Hiroko Morita-Lou. 1988. "Indicators of Science and Technology for Development." In Atul Wad ed., *Science, Technology, and Development*. Boulder, CO: Westview Press.

Armstrong, Adrienne. 1981. "The Political Consequences of Economic Dependence." *Journal of Conflict Resolution* 25 (3): 401-428.

Banks, Arthur S. 1981. "An Index of Socio-Economic Development 1869-1975." *Journal of Politics* 43 (3): 390-411.

Baran, Paul. 1957. *The Political Economy of Growth*. New York: Monthly Review.

Bath, Richard C., and Dilmus D. James. 1976. "Dependency Analysis of Latin America: Some Criticisms, Some Suggestions." *Latin American Research Review* 11 (3) 3-53.

Berry, William D., and Stanley Feldman. 1989. *Multiple Regression in Practice*. London: Sage.

Birdsall, Nancy. 1984. "Population Growth." *Finance and Development* September: 10-14.

Bodenheimer, Susanne. 1976. "The Ideology of Developmentalism: American Political Science's Paradigm Surrogate for Latin American Studies." *Berkeley Journal of Sociology* 15 (1): 95-137.

Bonilla, Robert, Andre G. Frank and Robert Girling eds. 1973. *Structures of Dependency*. Stanford, CA: Institute of Political Studies.

Bornschier, Volker. 1981. "Dependent Industrialization in the World Economy." *Journal of Conflict Resolution* 25 (3) September: 371-400.

Bornschier, Volker, and Thanh-Huyen Ballmer-Cao. 1979. "Income Inequality: A Cross-National Study of the Relationships Between MNC-Penetration, Dimensions of the Power Structure and Income Distribution." *American Sociological Review* 44: 487-506.

Bornschier, Volker, Christopher Chase-Dunn and Richard Rubinson. 1978. "Cross-National Evidence of the Effects of Foreign Investment and Aid on Economic Growth and Inequality: A Survey of Findings and a Reanalysis." *American Journal of Sociology* 84 (3): 651-683.

Bornschier, Volker, and Christopher Chase-Dunn. 1985. *Transnational Corporations and Underdevelopment*. New York: Praeger.

Brown, Michael B. 1974. *The Economics of Imperialism*. London: Penguin.

Caporaso, James A. 1978. "Dependence, Dependency, and Power in the Global System: a Structural and Behavioral Analysis." *International Organization* 32 (1): 13-43.

Cardoso, Fernando Henrique. 1973. "Associated Dependent Development: Theoretical and Practical Implications." In Alfred Stepan ed. *Authoritarian Brazil: Origin, Policy, and Future*. New Haven, CT: Yale University Press, 149-172.

Cardoso, Fernando, and Enzo Faletto. 1969. *Dependency and Development in Latin America*. Berkeley: University of California Press.

――― –. 1979. *Dependency and Development in Latin America*. Berkeley: University of California Press.

Chan, Steve, and Cal Clark. 1991. "Economic Growth and Popular Well-Being in Taiwan: A Time Series Examination of Some Preliminary Hypotheses." *The Western Political Quarterly* 44 (3) September: 560-582.

Chilcote, Ronald H., and Joel C. Edelstein. 1974. "Alternative Perspectives of Development and Underdevelopment in Latin America." In Chilcote and Edelstein eds., *Latin America: The Struggle With Dependency and Beyond*. New York: John Wiley and Sons, 1-87.

Cline, W. R. 1975. "Distribution and Development: A Survey of Literature." *Journal of Development Economics* 1: 359-400.

Cockroft, James D. 1974. "Mexico." In Ronald H. Chilcote and Joel C. Edelstein eds., *Latin America: The Struggle With Dependency and Beyond*. New York: John Wiley and Sons, 225-303.

Cockroft, James D., Andre Gunder Frank and Dale L. Johnson. 1974. *Dependence and Underdevelopment: Latin America's Political Economy*. New York: Doubleday.

Coleman, James S. 1965. *Education and Political Development*. Princeton, NJ: Princeton University Press.

Dasgupta, Partha. 1993. *An Inquiry into Well-Being and Destitution*. Oxford: Clarendon Press.

Dillard, Dudley. 1992. "Capitalism." In Charles K. Wilber and Kenneth P. Jameson eds. *The Political Economy of Development and Underdevelopment*. New York: McGraw-Hill.

Dolan, Michael B., and Brian W. Tomlin. 1980. "First World-Third World Linkages: External Relations and Economic Development." *International Organization* 34 (1) 441-463.

Donaldson, Thomas. 1991. "The Ethics of Conditionality in International Debt." *Millennium* 20 (2) Summer: 155-168.

Dos Santos, Theotonio. 1970. "The Structure of Dependence." *American Economic Review* 60 (1) May: 231-236.

――― . 1976. "The Crisis of Contemporary Capitalism." *Latin American*

Perspective 3 Spring: 84-99.

Duvall, Raymond. 1978. "Dependency and Dependencia Theory: Notes Towards Precision of Concept and Argument." *International Organization* 32 (1): 51-78.

Duvall, Raymond, Steven Jackson, Bruce Russett, Duncan Snidal, and David Sylvan. 1983. "A Formal Model of 'Dependencia' Theory: Structure and Measurement." In Bruce Russett and Richard Merritt, eds., *From National Development to Global Community*. New York: MacMillan.

Ellsworth, Paul T. 1969. *The International Economy*. New York: Macmillan.

Evans, Peter. 1976. "Continuities and Contradictions in the Evolution of Brazilian Dependence." *Latin American Perspectives* 3 Spring: 30-54.

———. 1979. *Dependent Development: The Alliance of Multinational, State, and Local Capital in Brazil*. Princeton, NJ: Princeton University Press.

———. 1983. "State, Local and Multinational Capital in Brazil: Prospects for the Stability of the 'Triple Alliance' in the Eighties." In Diana Tussie ed. *Latin America in the World Economy: New Perspectives*. New York: St. Martin's Press, 139-168.

Evans, Peter, and Michael Timberlake. 1980. "Dependence, Inequality, and the Growth of the Tertiary: A Comparative Analysis of Less Developed Countries." *American Sociological Review* 45 August: 531-552.

Fox, John. 1991. *Regression Diagnostics*. London: Sage.

Frank, Andre Gunder. 1967. *Capitalism and Underdevelopment in Latin America*. New York: Monthly Review Press.

———. 1969. *Latin America: Underdevelopment or Revolution*. New York: Monthly Review.

———. 1974. *Lumpenbourgeoisie: Lumpendevelopment, Dependence, Class and Politics in Latin America*. New York: Monthly Review Press.

Freedom House. 1973. "The Map of Freedom." *Freedom at Issue* 17 (3) January-February, 3.

Freund, Rudolf J. and Ramon C. Little. 1991. *SAS System for Regression*. Cary, NC: SAS Institute.

Friedman, Milton. 1981. *Capitalism and Freedom*. Chicago: University of Chicago Press.

———. 1982. "Free Markets and Generals." *Newsweek*. January 25: 59.

Furtado, Celso. 1958. "The External Disequilibrium in the Underdeveloped Economies." *Indian Journal of Economics* 38 (151) April: 398-410.

———. 1972. *Economic Development in Latin America*. Cambridge: Cambridge University Press.

Galtung, Johan. 1970. "Feudal Systems, Structural Violence and the Structural Theory of Revolutions." *IPRA: Studies in Peace Research Volume I*. Netherlands: Van Gorcum.

———. 1971. "A Structural Theory of Imperialism." *Journal of Peace Research*. 8: 81-119.

Gastil, Raymond. 1978, 1984, 1988, 1994. *Freedom in The World: Political*

Rights and Civil Liberties. Westport, CT: Greenwood Press.

Girvan, Norman. 1973. "The Development of Dependency Economics in the Caribbean and Latin America: Review and Comparison." *Social and Economic Studies* 22 (1) March: 434-461.

Gobalet, Jeanne G. and Larry J. Diamond. 1979. "Effects of Investment Dependence on Economic Growth." *International Studies Quarterly* 23 (3) September: 412-444.

Hartmann, Frederick H., and Robert L. Wendzel. 1994. *America's Foreign Policy in a Changing World*. New York: HarperCollins.

Hicks, Norman L., and Paul Streeten. 1975. "Indicators of Development: The Search for a Basic Needs Yardstick." *World Development* 7 (3): 567-580.

Huntington, Samuel. 1991. *The Third Wave*. Cambridge, MA: Harvard University Press.

Huntington, Samuel, and Joan Nelson. 1976. *No Easy Choice: Political Participation in Developing Countries*. Cambridge, MA: Harvard University Press.

Hveem, Helge. 1973. "The Global Dominance System." *Journal of Peace Research* 10 (4): 319-340.

Inkles, Alex, and David H. Smith. 1974. *Becoming Modern: Individual Change in Six Developing Countries*. Cambridge MA: Harvard University Press.

International Bank for Reconstruction and Development. 1974. *Finance and Development Volume II*. March.

International Monetary Fund. 1994. *Direction of Trade Yearbook*.

Jackman, Robert W. 1982. "Dependence on Foreign Investment and Economic Growth in the Third World." *World Politics* 34: 175-196.

Jackson, Steven I. 1979. "Capitalist Penetration: Concept and Measurement." *Journal of Peace Research* 16 (1): 41-55.

Johnson, Dale. 1973. *The Sociology of Change and Reaction in Latin America*. Indianapolis: Bobbs, Merrill.

Johnston, John. 1972 *Econometric Methods*. New York: McGraw-Hill.

Kaufman, Robert R., Harry I. Chernotsky and Daniel S. Geller. 1975. "A Preliminary Test of the Theory of Dependency." *Comparative Politics* 7: 303-330.

Kohli, Atul, Michael F. Altfeld, Saideh Lotfian and Russell Mardon. 1984. "Inequality in the Third World: An Assessment of Competing Explanations." *Comparative Political Studies* 17: 283-318.

Kuznets, Simon. 1955. "Economic Growth and Income Equality." *American Economic Review* 4 (5): 529-563.

Lall, Sanjaya. 1975. "Is Dependence a Useful Concept in Analyzing Underdevelopment? " *World Development* 3: 799-810.

Lenin, V. I. "Imperialism: The Highest Stage of Capitalism." 1960. In *V. I. Lenin, Selected Works in Three Volumes: Volume. 1*. Moscow: Foreign Languages Publishing House.

Leolegrande, William. 1979. "Cuban Dependency: A Comparison of Pre-Revolutionary and Post-Revolutionary International Economic Relations." *Cuban Studies* 9 (2) July: 7-28.

Lerner, Daniel. 1958. *The Passing of Traditional Society.* Glencoe, IL: Free Press.

Levy, Marion J. 1993. "Social Patterns (Structures) and Problems of Modernization." In Wilbert Moore and Robert M. Cook eds., *Readings on Social Change.* Englewood Cliffs, NJ: Prentice-Hall, 189-208.

Lipset, Seymour M. 1963. *Political Man: The Social Basis of Politics.* New York: Anchor Books.

———. 1959. "Some Social Requisites of Democracy." *American Political Science Review* 53 September: 534-577.

London, Bruce, and Williams, Bruce A. 1990. "National Politics, International Dependency, and Basic Needs Provision: A Cross-National Analysis." *Social Forces* 69 (2) December: 565-584.

Love, Joseph L. 1990. "Origins of Dependency Analysis." *Journal of Latin American Studies* 22 (1) February: 142-168.

Mahler, Vincent A. 1980. *Dependency Approaches to International Political Economy: A Cross-National Study.* New York: Columbia University Press.

Marx, Karl, and F. Engels. 1955. "Manifesto of the Communist Party." In S. Beer ed., *The Communist Manifesto.* New York: Appleton-Century-Crofts, 183-227.

Mayer, Lawrence C. 1989. *Redefining Comparative Politics.* Newbury Park, CA: Sage.

McClelland, David. 1967. *The Achieving Society.* New York: Free Press.

McGowan, Patrick J., and Dale L. Smith. 1978. "Economic Dependency in Black Africa: An Analysis of Competing Theories." *International Organization* 32 (1): 179-235.

McLaughlin, Martin M. 1979. *The United States and World Development: Agenda 1979.* New York: Praeger.

Mesa-Lago, Carmelo. 1981. *The Economy of Socialist Cuba: A Two-Decade Appraisal.* Albuquerque, NM: University of New Mexico Press.

Mitchell, William. 1988. "Virginia, Rochester, and Bloomington: Twenty-Five Years of Public Choice and Political Science." *Public Choice.* 56: 101-119.

Moore, Barrington. 1966. *The Social Origins of Dictatorship and Democracy: Land and Peasant in the Making of the Modern World.* Cambridge, MA: Harvard University Press.

Moran, Theodore H. 1978. "Multinational Corporations and Dependency: A Dialogue for Dependentistas and Non Dependentistas." *International Organization* 32 (1): 78-99.

Morris, Morris D. 1979. *Measuring the Condition of the World's Poor: The Physical Quality of Life Index.* New York: Pergamon Press.

Mosk, C., and S.R. Johansson. 1986. "Income and Mortality: Evidence from

Modern Japan." *Population and Development Review* 12: 415-440.

Munck, Ronaldo. 1985. *Politics and Dependence in the Third World.* London: Zed Press.

Mytelka, Lynn K. 1978. "Technological Dependence in the Andean Group." *International Organization* 32 (1): 100-139.

Nove, Alec. 1975. "On Reading Andre Gunder Frank." In Oxaal, Ivar, Tony Barnett, and David Booth eds., *Beyond the Sociology of Development: Economy and Society in Latin America and Africa.* London: Routledge and Kegan Paul, 440-470.

O'Brien, Philip. 1975. "A Critique of Latin American Theories of Dependency." In Oxaal, Ivar, Tony Barnett, and David Booth eds., *Beyond the Sociology of Development: Economy and Society in Latin America and Africa.* London: Routledge and Kegan Paul, 7-27.

O'Donnell, Guillermo. 1973. *Modernization and Bureaucratic-Authoritarianism: Studies in South American Politics.* Berkeley: Institute of International Studies, University of California.

OECD. 1978. *Development Cooperation, 1978 Review.* Paris: OECD.

O'Hearn, Denis. 1989. "The Irish Case of Dependency: An Exception to the Exceptions? " *American Sociological Review* 54 August: 578-596.

Olson, Mancur. 1963. "Rapid Growth as a Destabilizing Force." *Journal of Economic History* 23 (4) December: 529-552.

Ostrom, Charles W. 1991. *Time Series Analysis: Regression Techniques.* Second Ed. London: Sage.

Owens, Edgar. 1987. *The Future of Freedom in the Developing World.* New York: Pergamon Press.

Packenham, Robert A. 1986. "Capitalist Dependency and Socialist Dependency." *Journal of InterAmerican Studies and World Affairs* 28 (1) Spring: 59-91.

Papanek, Gustav F. 1978. "Aid, Foreign Private Investment, Savings, and Growth In Less Developed Countries." *Journal of Political Economy* 81 (1): 120-130.

Paukert, Felix. 1973. "Income Distribution at Different Levels of Development: A Survey of Evidence." *International Labor Review* 108: 97-125.

Payer, Cheryl. 1974. *The Debt Trap.* Middlesex England: Penguin.

Petras, James ed. 1973. *Latin America: From Dependence to Revolution.* New York: John Wiley and Sons.

Pourgerami, Abbas. 1991. *Development and Democracy in the Third World.* Boulder, CO: Westview Press.

Prebisch, Raul. 1950. *The Economic Development of Latin America and Its Principal Problems.* New York: United Nations.

———. 1961. "Economic Development or Monetary Stability: The False Dilemma." *Economic Bulletin for Latin America* 6 (1) March: 7-38.

———. 1964. *Towards a New Trade Policy for Development.* New York: United Nations.

Przewarski, Adam, and Henry Teune. 1970. *The Logic of Comparative Social*

Inquiry. New York: Wiley.

Pye, Lucian. 1966. *Aspects of Political Development.* Boston: Little, Brown.

Rapkin, David P. 1976. "The World-Economy and the Distribution of Income Within States: A Cross-National Study." *American Sociological Review* 41 August: 638-659.

Ravenhill, John. 1986. "Inequality in the Third World." *Comparative Political Studies* 19 July: 259-268.

Ray, David. 1973. "The Dependency Model of Latin American Underdevelopment: Three Basic Fallacies." *Journal of InterAmerican Studies and World Affairs* XV (1) February: 4-20.

Ray, James Lee, and Thomas Webster. 1978. "Dependency and Economic Growth in Latin America." *International Studies Quarterly* 22 (3): 409-435.

Rostow, Walt W. 1964. "The Takeoff into Self-Sustained Growth." In Amitai Etzioni and Eva Etzioni eds., *Social Change.* New York: Basic Books, 285-300.

Rubinson, Richard. 1977. "Dependence, Government Revenue, and Economic Growth, 1955-1970." *Comparative International Development* 12: 3-29.

Sayrs, Lois W. 1989. *Pooled Time Series Analysis.* Newbury Park, CA: Sage.

Schmitter, Philippe E. 1971. "Desarrollo Retrasado, Dependencia Externa y Cambio Politico en America Latina." *Foro Internacional.* 12 December: 135-174.

Sklar, Richard. 1987. "Postimperialism: A Class Analysis of Multinational Corporate Expansion." In David G. Becker, Jeff Frieden, Sayre P. Schatz, and Richard L. Sklar eds., *Postimperialism: International Capitalism and Development in the Late Twentieth Century.* Boulder, CO: Lynne Rienner Publishers.

Smelser, Neil. 1964. "Toward a Theory of Modernization." In Amitai and Eva Etzioni eds., *Social Change.* New York: Basic Books, 268-284.

Smith, Adam. 1776. *Inquiry Into the Nature and Causes of the Wealth of Nations.* Oxford: Oxford University Press.

Snider, D.A. 1971. *Introduction to International Economics.* Homewood, IL: Irwin.

So, Alvin Y. 1990. *Social Change and Development.* Newbury Park, CA: Sage.

Sofranko, Andrew J., Michael F. Nolan and Robert C. Bealer. 1975. "Energy Use and Alternative Measures of Societal Modernity." *Sociology and Social Research* 59 (3) July: 301-317.

Spero, Joan Edelman. 1990. *The Politics of International Economic Relations.* New York: St. Martin's Press.

Staniland, Martin. 1985. *What Is Political Economy? A Study of Social Theory and Underdevelopment.* New Haven, CT: Yale University Press.

Stevenson, Paul. 1972. "External Economic Variables Influencing the Economic Growth Rate of Seven Major Latin American Nations." *Canadian Review of Sociology and Anthropology* 9 (4): 347-356.

Stewart, Francis. 1985. *Basic Needs in Developing Countries*. Baltimore: Johns
    Hopkins University Press.

Stimson, James A. 1985. "Regression in Space and Time: A Statistical Essay."
    American Journal of Political Science (29): 914-947.

Stoneman, Colin. 1976. "Foreign Capital and Economic Growth." *World
    Development* 3 (1): 11-26.

Szymanski, Albert. 1976. "Dependence, Exploitation and Economic Growth."
    Journal of Political and Military Sociology (4) Spring: 53-65.

Tyler, William G., and Peter J. Wogart. 1973. "Economic Dependence and
    Marginalization: Some Empirical Evidence." *Journal of InterAmerican
    Studies and World Affairs*. Vol. 15, 36-46.

United Nations Development Programme. 1990. *Human Development Report*.
    New York: Oxford University Press.

West, Robert L. 1973. "Economic Dependence and Policy in Developing
    Countries." In C. Fred Bergsten and William G. Tyler eds., *Leading
    Issues in International Economic Policy*. Lexington, MA: D.C. Heath,
    157-183.

Wimberley, Dale W. 1990. "Investment Dependence and Alternative
    Explanations of Third World Mortality: A Cross-National Study."
    American Sociological Review Vol. 55, No. 1, February, 75-91.

World Bank. 1994. *Social Development Indicators*. Washington, DC: World
    Bank.

World Bank. 1994. *World Development Indicators*. 1994. Washington, DC:
    World Bank.

World Intellectual Property Organization. 1994. *World Industrial Properties
    Statistics*. Washington, DC.

Young, Frank. 1990. "Do Some Authoritarian Governments Foster Physical
    Quality of Life?" *Social Indicators Research* 22 June: 351-366.

Index

aid, 7, 8, 10-11, 37, 40, 52, 65, 67, 72,
73, 76, 79, 81, 83-84, 87, 91, 93,
96-97, 104, 106, 110, 113, 117-118,
123
and dependency, 23, 35-36, 41, 44-
45, 52, 116, 119
and economic development, 61
and economic power dependency,
34
and factor analysis, 72-73
and GNP, 111
and growth, 8, 10
and human rights, 52
and ideology, 52
and inequality, 52
and investment dependency, 36
and the liberal paradigm, 8, 10-11,
38-39
and poverty, 91
and PQLI, 45, 84-87, 110-113, 119,
123
and primary exports, 77, 80, 86
and profit repatriation, 34
and political factors, 52
and Quality Improvement, 57, 84-
88, 116, 119-125
and regime types, 52, 117
and sovereignty, 52
in bivariate analysis, 74-77, 90,
111, 123
in multivariate analysis, 92-100,
110, 117, 123-124
measurement of, 52
Almond, Gabriel, 1, 11, 15, 25, 26
Alschuler, L.R., 2, 33, 41
Anandakrishnan, M., 53
Apter, David, 10.
associated-dependent development, 19,
20, 22, 60, 80, 109
authoritarian regimes, 2, 5, 16-17, 19,
21, 23, 29, 32, 45, 59-61, 72, 76,

79, 93-94, 99, 107, 117-118, 120,
124-125
autocorrelation, 65-66, 92, 95-98, 105,
107
correcting for, 98-99
B coefficients, 73, 91-95, 99, 111-116,
122
balance of payments, 13
Ballmer-Cao, Thanh-Huyen, 33, 38, 41,
55-56, 62
Banks, Arthur S., 61
Baran, Paul, 18
Bath, Richard, 7, 14-19, 24, 49, 94
Bealer, Robert C., 54-55
Berry, William, 65
beaureaucratic authoritarianism, 2, 19,
23, 72
Birdsall, Nancy, 64
birth rates, 35
bivariate analysis, 71, 73-74, 77, 81-84,
86, 88, 90, 92-93, 96, 104, 111,
117, 119, 121-123
of control and dependent variables,
77-78
of dependency and control
variables, 76-77
of independent variables, 74-75
statistical significance of, 74-75
Bodenheimer, Susan, 19, 20
Bonilla, Robert, 19, 55
Bornschier, Volker, 2, 4, 33, 36, 38-41,
45, 48, 51, 55-56, 61-62, 72, 106,
115
bourgeoisie, 5, 16, 22, 26, 55, 86
and authoritarian rule, 17
domestic sector, 16
international sector, 16, 17, 55, 86
Brown, Michael, 25
capital, 7-8, 10, 12, 16, 19-23, 34, 37-
38, 40-41, 45-46, 49-52, 62, 72, 79,
100, 113

flows of, 7, 8, 14
penetration of, 51, 52
capital dependency, 37, 53
capitalism, 7, 11, 17, 26-27, 31, 59
   and democracy, 59, 85
   and productivity, 18
   and underdevelopment, 18
   contradictions in, 27
capitalist, 1, 5, 9, 11, 13-20, 26-27, 30, 37, 40, 53, 121, 125
Caporaso, James, 30-33, 72, 90
Cardoso, Fernando, 3-5, 17-21, 24-25, 29-30, 32, 51-52, 55, 60, 63-64, 76, 80, 82, 88, 90, 93, 101, 104-105, 107, 109, 114-119, 122, 124
causal relationships, 2, 4, 35, 37-39, 44-45, 54, 61, 85, 90, 91
center, 6, 15, 18-19, 22
Chan, Steve, 56
Chase-Dunn, Christopher, 33-34, 36,-38, 41, 51, 56
Chernotsky, Harry, 37, 41
Chilcoate, Ronald H., 15-18, 23-24, 47-52, 55-56, 71, 74, 84, 112-114, 116
civic culture, 11
Clark, Cal, 56
class, 15, 18-19, 21, 23, 27, 30, 85, 86, 118
clientelism, 18, 22, 46
Cline, W.R., 7,8, 113, 116
Cockroft, James, 14, 18
coercive authoritarianism, 32
Coleman, James, 10
colonialism, 12, 14-15, 17, 22
commodity concentration, 35, 39-41
Communist bloc, 1, 26, 65, 71
comparative advantage, 8, 21, 125
contradictions in capitalism, 11
control variables, 2-5, 12, 16, 20-23, 26, 35-41, 43-45, 48-53, 59, 61-65, 67-68, 71, 74, 76-77, 80-83, 85-93, 96-100, 103-119, 121-124
core, 12-16, 18-27, 32, 34-35, 44-52, 62, 65, 67-69, 72-73, 75-77, 83-84, 86-87, 91, 93, 95-100, 104, 106, 109-110, 112-113, 116-118, 121-123
correlation analysis, 40, 66, 74-77, 79-83, 86, 88, 92, 95, 97-99, 105, 107

cross-sectional analysis, 2, 3, 31, 36, 38, 47, 61, 65
culture, 11, 26, 101, 125
Dagsputa, Partha, 57
Darwin, Charles, 7, 9
debt, 25, 32, 35, 37, 40-41, 44, 49-52, 61, 67,-68, 73, 75-76, 79, 81, 83-84, 86-87, 91, 93, 95-97, 99, 104, 106, 110-111, 113-115, 117-118, 123
decapitalization, 51
democracy, 1, 5, 10, 11
   and aid, 77
   and capitalism, 11, 59, 85
   and civic culture, 11
   and collectivization, 59-60
   and economic development, 10, 59-60, 80, 85, 124
   and GNP per capita, 85
   and PQLI, 85
   and radical dependency, 115
   and raw material exports, 77
   and trade partner concentration, 77
dependency 1-125
   and aid, 35, 37-38, 40, 52, 80
   and area, 63
   and authoritarian regimes, 19-22, 59-61, 76-77, 79
   and capital drain, 23
   and capitalism, 17
   and class struggle, 15, 20, 23, 46, 64, 86
   and clientelism, 46, 68
   and colonialism, 12, 22
   and debt, 35, 49-50
   and democracy, 60, 76, 77
   and development, 2-3, 6, 18, 22-23, 43, 44, 56, 71, 79, 124-125
   and direct foreign investment, 40, 51, 52, 68
   and economic growth, 3-5, 13, 19, 27, 33-37, 40, 44, 47, 54, 60-62, 64-69, 105, 109, 121, 124, 125
   and energy, 50
   and exploitation, 11-12, 26
   and export commodity concentration, 40
   and external factors, 88
   and GNP, 35, 81
   and GNP growth, 63
   and GNP per capita, 35, 44, 54, 62,

65, 68, 79-80, 84-85, 90-92
and GNP per capita growth, 44, 46,
   55, 63, 65, 68, 81-84
and imperialism, 11, 18
and independent variables, 89
and inequality, 3-4, 21-24, 27, 33,
   36-37, 39-41, 44-46, 52, 54, 56, 60-
   69, 72, 79, 83-86, 90, 103-108, 109,
   114, 121, 125
and inequality growth, 103, 108
and internal factors, 26, 39, 85, 88
and liberal theory, 7, 9, 11, 25, 44-
   45, 54, 64, 88, 92, 114, 115, 121
and Marxism, 11-12, 25-26, 121
and multinational corporations, 21,
   33
and neocolonialism, 12
and nonfuel primary products in
   exports, 49, 80
and patents, 53
and physical quality of life, 3-5, 21-
   22, 27, 58, 61, 109
and political unrest, 24
and popultion growth, 77
and profit repatriation, 34
and PQLI, 4-5, 33, 45, 58-59, 61-
   68, 81, 84, 86, 109-116, 121
and PQLI growth, 4-5, 33, 45-46,
   58-59, 62-68, 84-88, 90, 109-110,
   121-122
and Quality Improvement, 4-5, 58-
   59, 64, 81, 86, 89, 109-124
and quality of life, 68-69
and regime type, 5, 68, 76-77, 81,
   114, 117
and socialist revolution, 15, 18, 22-
   24, 85
and sovereignty, 50
and spurious relationships, 43, 112
and technological independence, 80
and trade, 11, 37-38, 47, 80
and trade partner concentration, 40,
   48, 62, 80
and trade sanctions, 48
and trade with core nations, 47-48
and tertiarty employment, 39
and underdevelopment, 15, 24-26,
   54, 69, 74, 79, 86
and unequal exchange, 15, 17, 24,
   24, 38, 49, 72, 82, 85, 86

and wealth, 54-55, 62, 109, 121
as a continuous variable, 25, 29, 33
as a dichotomy, 25, 29, 33
as propaganda, 25
as a one-dimensional concept, 46,
   72, 75
as a multi-dimensional concept, 46,
   72, 75, 88, 121
as a tautology, 27
asymmetric properties of, 31-32
bivariate analysis of, 74-75, 111,
   121
capital dependency, 100
case studies in, 40
concrete situations of, 31
criticisms of, 24-25
cultural, 32
definition of, 16, 43
dependent development, 79
dependent variables of, 54
dialectical analysis of, 30, 31
empirical analysis of, 2-4, 7, 30, 33-
   37, 41, 43-44, 51, 55-56, 61-67, 71-
   125
energy dependency, 41, 50-51, 81
expected relationships, 71
factor analysis of, 71-73
historical-structural analysis of, 29-
   31
holistic, 90
in black Africa, 34
in socialist countries, 40
incompleteness of previous
   analysis, 2-5, 33-38, 59
independent variables of, 46-53
investment dependency, 36-37, 40,
   51
literature, 1, 2, 6, 7, 11-41, 46-52,
   61-63, 72, 76, 89, 112-120
measurement of, 24, 29, 31-38, 40,
   46-66
multivariate analysis of, 82, 89-119
new dependency, 19-24, 51, 82,
   101, 105
operationalization of, 26, 67-68
origins, 7, 11-14
radical literature, 14-19, 55, 100
secondary usages of, 32
socialist dependency, 25, 40
technological, 16, 22, 32, 37, 40, 53

testing of, 2, 29, 89, 121
dependent development, 114
  and elites, 114
  and masses, 114
dependent growth, 4, 21, 25, 60, 115,
  119
dependent variables, 31
  in empirical analysis, 71-124
  in empirical literature, 34-44
  operationalization of, 54-67
descriptive analysis, 30
development, 1, 2, 10, 25-29, 35, 69,
  79, 121
  and aid, 52-53, 62
  and capitalism, 11
  and culture, 11
  and debt, 37, 49-50
  and democracy, 10, 59
  and dependency, 2-6, 30-31, 72, 76,
    79-84, 125
  and dependency literature, 13-25,
    43, 46, 79-82, 84, 88, 90, 92, 94,
    112, 114, 116, 118, 122, 124
  and direct foreign investment, 37
  and energy dependency, 50
  and inequality, 79-84, 114, 116,
    118, 124
  and liberal theory, 7, 12, 92, 121
  and personalities, 11
  and regime types, 60-61, 79-80, 93-
    94, 124
  and technological independence,
    53-54
  and trade concentration, 112
  and values, 11
  as a continuum 10
  as equality, 23, 55-56
  as GNP per capita, 55
  as PQLI, 57-58
  crises of, 10
  empirical analysis of, 32-33, 36-38,
    71-125
  external causes of, 71, 88
  goals of, 3
  in literature, 1, 6
  in Marxist theory, 26
  internal causes of, 10-11, 17, 114
  stages of, 10
determinism, 19, 21
Diamond, Larry, 33, 46, 55, 62

Dillard, Dudley, 8-9
direct foreign investment, 3, 12, 25-26,
  62, 67
  and consumer demand, 8
  and debt, 37
  and development, 26
  and growth, 8, 19, 35, 38, 96, 100,
    124
  and inequality, 4, 7-8, 14, 36, 38-
    39, 45, 106, 115, 124
  and liberal theory, 7-8, 44-45
  and PQLI, 115
  and technology transfer, 8, 40
  and unemployment, 39
  and wealth, 35, 62
  as a dependency indicator, 34, 41,
    51-52
  flows of, 106
  in bivariate analysis, 75, 86
  in dependency literature, 17-19, 51
  in empirical studies, 34-41, 68
  in factor analysis, 73
  in multivariate analysis, 96, 100,
    106, 124
  stocks of, 106
Dolan, Michael, 8, 32-33, 39, 45, 48,
  51-52, 55, 57, 62
domestic capital formation, 37, 41
Donaldson, Thomas, 50
Dos Santos, Theotonio, 15-16, 22-23,
  29, 51-52
Durbin-Watson statistic, 66, 91-93, 95-
  96, 98, 105, 107, 110, 113, 117, 119
Dummy variables, 66, 98-99
Duvall, Raymond, 29-32, 51, 72, 90
economic colonies, 17-18
economic growth. See GNP per capita
  growth
economic market dependency, 34
economic power dependency, 34
Edelstein, Joel C., 15-18, 23-24, 47-52,
  55-56, 71, 74, 84, 112-114, 116
Ellsworth, Paul, 7, 85, 116
energy consumption per capita, 55
energy dependency, 41, 50-51, 67-68,
  71, 73, 75-76, 79, 81, 83, 87, 91,
  93, 96-97, 106, 110, 113, 117-118,
  123
  and dependency theory, 79, 100
  and Quality Improvement, 87

and technological independence, 74
and trade concentration, 74
in bivariate analysis, 74
in factor analysis, 71, 73
in multivariate analysis, 124
Engels, Frederick, 26-27
Evans, Peter, 2, 9-24, 32, 39, 41, 51,
    56, 79, 82
external causes of development, 5, 10,
    13, 15-16, 19-20, 21, 23-24, 30, 32,
    39, 47, 49-52, 59, 63, 68, 71-75, 82,
    88, 94, 100, 103, 113, 125
external public debt, 37-40
factor analysis, 47-52, 66, 71-72, 88,
    121
Faletto, Enzo, 3-5, 17-21, 24-25, 29-30,
    32, 51-52, 55, 60, 63-64, 76, 80, 82,
    88, 90, 93, 101, 104-105, 107, 109,
    114-119, 122, 124
Feldman, Stanley, 65-66
flows, 38-39, 66
Fox, John, 65
Frank, Andre Gunder, 11, 14-19, 22-27,
    48, 54-56, 61, 112, 115
Freedom House, 60-61
Friedman, Milton, 59-60, 99
Galtung, Johan, 18, 35, 46, 48
Geller, David, 37, 41
Generalized Least Squares
    Autoregressive Moving Average,
    65-66, 91, 98
Gini index, 37, 41, 56-57
Girling, Robert, 19, 55-56
Girvan, Norman, 12-13
GNP, 34-36, 38, 47, 97
    and area, 77
    and dependency, 112
    and direct foreign investment, 35
    and energy consumption per capita,
    35
    and GNP per capita, 82
    and GNP per capita growth, 82
    and inequality, 83
    and foreign penetration, 56
    and monoculture, 62
    and PQLI, 85, 111, 115
    and primary exports, 83
    and Quality Improvement, 88, 119,
    120
    and technological independence, 77

as a control variable, 36, 38, 40, 63-
    64, 67-68, 81, 83-84, 87, 93, 97,
    105-106, 113, 115, 117-120, 123
growth of, 34
in bivariate analysis, 77
in factor analysis, 72
GNP per capita, 35, 85, 87, 123
    and aid, 80, 91-93
    and area, 80
    and democracy, 93and GNP, 80
    and dependency, 35, 44, 54, 80, 91-
    94, 100, 120
    and GNP, 80
    and GNP per capita growth, 82, 99
    and inequality, 79
    and mortality rates, 61
    and population growth, 34, 80
    and PQLI, 62, 80, 85, 114
    and PQLI growth, 81
    and primary exports, 80, 82, 92-97
    96
    and Quality Improvement, 80, 88,
    119
    and quality of life, 58
    and regime types, 79-80, 85, 93-94,
    124
    and technological independence,
    79-80
    and trade concentration, 80, 92-93
    and underdevelopment, 2, 56
    as a control variable, 61-68, 83, 97,
    99, 117, 119
    as a dependent variable, 54, 67-68,
    83
    as economic development, 5, 37,
    41, 55, 58
    as wealth, 54
    bivariate analysis of, 79-81, 119
    descriptive statistics of, 89-91
    explanation of variance in, 92
    in dependency literature, 2, 35, 37,
    56, 79, 81, 84, 91
    multivariate analysis of, 89-94
GNP per capita growth, 35, 81
    and area, 82
    and control variables, 97
    and debt, 99
    and dependency, 2, 44, 46, 55, 81-
    84, 97-99, 107, 124
    and GNP, 82

and GNP per capita, 62, 82, 100
and inequality, 45, 82, 84, 105, 107
and population growth, 82
and PQLI, 82, 115
and PQLI growth, 82
and primary exports, 81,, 82, 92,
    95-97
and Quality Improvement, 119
and regime type, 82, 108
and trade partner concentration, 95,
    99, 124
and trade with the core, 95, 99, 122
as a control variable, 45, 62-63, 117
as economic development, 5
bivariate analysis of, 80-81
descriptive statistics of, 90-91, 95
in empirical studies, 34, 38, 55
multivariate analysis of, 64, 65, 82,
    89, 94-101
goals of anlaysis,3-6
Gobalet, Jeanne, G, 33, 46, 55, 62
growth, See GNP per capita growth
growth/equity trade-off, 45, 117
heteroskedasticity, 65-66
Hicks, Norman, 56
historical approach, 12, 20
Hirschman, Albert, 11-12
Hveem, Helge, 53
Huntington, Samuel, 1, 4, 45, 64, 8
hypothesis #1, 17, 99-101
hypothesis #2, 17, 105, 108, 122
hypothesis #3, 17, 112-115, 117-118,
    120, 122
imperialism, 11, 14-16, 18
import substitution, 12-14, 21, 50
importance of research, 5, 68
independent variables, 37, 39, 41, 46,
    56, 58-59, 66, 115
bivariate analysis of, 74-75, 83
factor analysis of, 71
interrelationships among, 72
multivariate analysis of, 89, 95, 109
industrialization, 8, 12, 17, 20-22, 50
inequality, 22, 55-56
and aid, 45, 52
and area, 107
and associated-dependent develop-
    ment, 82, 114
and bivariate analysis, 83
and cultural factors, 106

and debt, 123
and democracy, See regime type
and dependency, 33, 35-57, 45, 46,
    56, 64, 90, 104-105, 107, 118, 124
and direct foreign investment, 4, 36,
    106, 115
and economic growth, 3, 24, 27, 37,
    64, See also GNP per capita growth
and external factors, 63
and GNP, 83
and GNP per capita, 79, 80, 83-83
and GNP per capita growth, 82-84
and governmental policies, 105
and historical factors, 105
and penetration by multinational
    corporations, 4, 38-39, 41, 45, 105-
    106
and PQLI, 3, 64, 84, 86, 114
and PQLI growth, See Quality
Improvement
and political economic policies, 106
and primary exports, 83, 104-105
and Quality Improvement, 64, 83-
    84, 88, 118
and quality of life, 4, 5, See also
PQLI
and regime type, 5, 45, 60-61, 107,
    124
and unequal exchange, 31
as a control variable, 63, 124
and development, 22
average measure of, 104
bivariate analysis of, 82-84
descriptive statistics of, 103-104
in dependency literature, 2-5, 20,
    24, 79
in developed economies, 9
in empirical studies, 36-38, 41, 45,
    56-57, 63-64
incompleteness of data on, 105, 108

measurement of, 37, 41, 56, 57,
    103, multivariate analysis of, 103-
    108, 114, 118, 122-124
range of, 103
valid cases of, 103
infant mortality, 27, 58, 71, 109, 113
interdependence, 16, 35
interest groups, 59
internal causes of development, 10

International Bank for Reconstruction and Development, 13-14.
Intervening variables, 38, 39
investment, 8, 10, 17, 26
investment dependency, 36-38, 41
Jackman, Robert, 33, 35-36, 55
Jackson, Steven, 6, 40, 47, 51-53, 62, 72, 74
James, Dilmus, 7, 14-19, 24, 49, 94
Johansson, S.R., 61-62
Johnson, Dale, 14-15, 18, 23, 56
Kaufman, Robert R., 2, 33-37, 41, 48, 51, 56, 64, 72-73
Keynes, John Maynard, 9
Kohli, Atul, 36, 105-106
Kuznets, Simon, 4
Lall, Sanjaya, 25-26
Lenin, Vladimir, 1, 11, 14-16, 26
Leolegrande, William, 40, 47-48, 50, 52
Lerner, Daniel, 11, 14
Levy, Marion, 10
liberal paradigm, 1, 7, 44, 121
    and aid, 8, 116
    and debt, 96, 99
    and dependency, 44
    and direct foreign investment, 12
    and economic growth, 44
    and inequality, 7-8, 45, 87, 114
    and investment, 8, 12, 45
    and physical quality of life, 64
    and population growth, 114
    and PQLI, 85, 114
    and policy, 125
    and primary exports, 92
    and Quality Improvement, 88, 116, 119
    and regime type, 60, 80, 124
    and technological independence, 54
    and trade, 8, 13, 44
    criticisms of, 9, 18-21, 121
Lipset, S.M., 10, 59, 80, 85, 94, 115, 117, 124.
life expectancy, 27, 57-58, 60-61, 71, 109, 113
literacy, 27, 57-58, 61, 109, 113
loans, 7-8, 50
loan conditions, 50
London, Bruce, 51

longitudinal analysis, 2-3, 5, 32, 36-37, 57, 105-106
Love, Joseph, 12, 24, 40, 98
lower classes, 3, 8-9, 16, 58, 60, 64, 85, 114-116, 118, 120
Mahler, Vincent, 72
managerial bourgeoisie, 21-22
marginalization, 39, 63
Marx, Karl, 1, 9, 11-12, 25-26, 121
mass communication 10, 15, 26
Mayer, Lawrence, 15, 26-27
McClelland, David, 14
McGowan, Patrick, 2, 33-35, 41, 48-49, 51-52, 55
McLaughlin, Martin, 57-58
mercantilism, 16
Mesa-Lago, Carmelo, 40, 47-52
metropolis, 15-17, 48
Micro-Crunch, 65-66
Mitchell, William, 59-60
MNCs. See multinational corporations
modernization perspective. See liberal theory
monoculture, 51, 62
monopoly, 16
Moran, Theodore, 9
Morita-Lou, H., 53
Morris, Morris D., 57-58
Mosk, C., 61-62
multicolinearity, 65-66
multinational corporations, 2, 21-22, 26, 32, 36
    and dependency, 1, 21-22, 29, 32-33, 51
    and inequality, 36, 38, 41, 106
    fresh investment of, 39
    indirect effects of, 38
    penetration of, 4, 38-39, 45, 105
Munck, Ronaldo, 20-21
Myrdal, Gunnar, 11-14
Mytelka, Lynn, 40
nationaliztion of industries, 21, 38
Nazi trade policy, 12
Nelson, Joan, 4, 45, 64
neocolonialism, 12, 22, 100
new dependency, 19-24, 50-51, 82, 100-101, 105
Nolan, Michael F., 54-55, 107, 109, 114-115

nonfuel primary product exports, 19
    and aid, 75
    75-90, 104, 111, 124
    and dependency, 49, 51, 85, 90, 92,
        94, 107-108, 111, 113, 117-118,
        123-124
    and economic growth, 35
    and factor analysis, 73
    and GNP, 77
    and GNP per capita, 80, 82, 92, 94,
        96-97, 100, 124
    and GNP per capita growth, 81, 94,
        96-97, 100, 124
    and inequality, 83, 104-107
    and PQLI, 85-86
    and Quality Improvement, 124
    and unequal exchange, 49, 100
    as an independent variable, 49, 67-
        68, 79, 81-84, 87, 91, 93
    measurement of, 49
Nove, Alec, 25
O'Brien, Phillip, 25
O'Donnell, Guillermo, 20-21, 24, 46,
    60, 76, 80, 107, 115, 118, 124
O'Hearne, Denis, 50
Olson, Mancur, 4, 59-60
operationalization, 66-67
ordinary least squares residual
    variance, 65
Overseas Development Council, 57
Ostrom, Charles, 64-65, 98-99
overview of operations, 66-67
Owens, Edgar, 60-61
Packenham, Robert, 25, 40, 47-4850-
    53, 72
Papanek, Gustav, 2
patent and trademark registration, 40,
    53, 67-68, 73, 75-76, 91, 93, 96-97,
    100, 104, 106, 113, 117-118
path analysis, 38
Paukert, Felix, 37
Pearson product moment correlations,
    73, 79-81
periphery, 12-15, 18-22, 24-26, 35, 44,
    46-51, 56, 62, 69, 86, 91, 99, 112-
    113, 115-117, 119
Petras, James, 15, 18, 23
policy implications, 69, 112, 120, 125

pooled cross-sectional analysis, 65-66,
    68, 89, 91-93, 95-98, 103-106, 110,
    112-113, 115-119
pooled regressions. See pooled cross-
    sectional analysis
population growth, 45
    and aid. See aid
    and area. See area
    and consumption, 62
    and debt. See debt
    and dependencey. See dependency
    and energy independence. See
        energy independence
    and GNP. See GNP
    and GNP per capita. See GNP per
        capita
    and GNP per capita growth. See
        GNP per capita growth
    and inequality. See inequality
    and PQLI. See PQLI
    and primary exports. See primary
        exports
    and Quality Improvement. See
        Quality Improvement
    and regime type. See regime type
    as a control variable, 62
populist authoritarian regimes, 60, 116-
    119
Pourgerami, Abbas, 5, 45, 64.
PQLI, 33
    and aid, 45 84, 87, 111-113, 119,
        124
    and area, 85, 112
    and debt, 85, 110, 113-114
    and democracy, 85
    and dependency, 4-5, 33, 45, 64-65,
        68, 81, 83-87, 90, 109-125
    and direct foreign investment, 85,
        115
    and energy independence, 85, 124
    and GNP, 85, 111-115
    and GNP per capita, 62, 68, 80, 87,
        114
    and inequality, 5, 64, 85-86, 114,
        124
    and liberal theory, 82, 85, 112, 114,
        124
    and natural disasters, 43
    and population growth, 85, 112,
        114, 119

and primary exports, 85-86, 111-112
and Quality Improvement, 64-65, 81, 84, 86
and regime types, 85, 114, 124
and technological independence, 85, 124
and trade concentration, 85, 87, 111-112, 117-118, 122
and unequal exchange, 111-114
as a control variable, 64, 79, 112
as a dependent variable, 59, 68-69, 110-116
bivariate analysis of, 84-86, 111
descriptive statistics of, 109
explanation of index, 109-110
in empirical studies, 33
measurement of, 57-59, 65, 71, 109
multivariate analysis of, 65, 109-115
PQLI growth. *See* Quality Improvement
Prebisch, Raul, 11-14, 24, 49-50.
profit repatriation, 34
Przeworski, Adam, 31
Pye, Lucian, 10
Quality Improvement, 4
and aid, 84-88, 117, 119, 124-125
and area, 86, 88, 119
and dependency. *See* dependency
and direct foreign investment, 124
and empirical studies, 33
and energy independence, 87, 124
and GNP, 88
and GNP per capita, 62, 80, 87, 119
and GNP per capita growth, 82, 119, 121, 124
and inequality, 86, 118-119, 123
and population growth, 87-88, 114, 119
and PQLI, *See* PQLI
and primary exports, 86, 124
and regime type, 87, 117-120
and technological independence, 124
and trade concentration, 87, 112, 117-119, 123
as a control variable, 64, 79
biavariate analysis of, 79-87, 119, 124

descriptive statistics of, 116
measurement of, 59, 65, 115-116
multivariate analysis of, 65, 68, 115-120
valid cases of, 115
quality of life, 21, 27
Rapkin, David, 35
Ravenhill, John, 36
Ray, David, 25-26
Ray, James Lee, 33-34
regime type, 59
Remmer, Karen, 60-61
residual variance ratio, 98
Rostow, W.W., 10
rotated factor matrix, 72-73
Rubinson, Richard, 2, 33, 36-37, 41, 43, 48
sample, 71
satellite, 15
Sayrs, Lois, 64-65
Schmitter, Philippe, 47, 51-52, 72
Schumpeter, Joseph, 85
Sklar, Richard, 21-22
Smelser, Neil, 10-11
Smith, Adam, 8-9
Smith, Dale, 2, 33-35, 41, 48-52, 55
Snider, D.A., 7-8, 45, 85, 114
So, Alvin, 10, 18
Sofranko, Andrew J., 54-55
Spencer, Herbert, 9
Spero, Joan, 50
spurious relationships, 43
stage development, 9-10, 16-17, 25
state as unified actor, 30
Stanilind, Martin, 20
Stevenson, Paul, 2, 41
Stewart, Francis, 61-62
Stimson, James, 66, 98
Stoneman, Colin, 2, 33-34, 51
Streeten, Paul, 56
structural distortions, 30
Szymanski, 2, 33-34, 41, 51-52
takeoff, 10
tariffs, 1, 13, 48, 50, 60
technological dependency
and aid. *See* aid
and area. *See* area
and consumption, 62
and debt. *See* debt
and dependencey. *See* dependency

and energy independence. *See* energy independence
and GNP. *See* GNP
and GNP per capita. *See* GNP per capita
and GNP per capita growth. *See* GNP per capita growth
and inequality. *See* inequality
and PQLI. *See* PQLI
and primary exports. *See* primary exports
and Quality Improvement. *See* Quality Improvement
and regime type. *See* regime type
as a control variable, 62.
See also patents
tertiary unemployment, 39
Teune, Henry, 31
Timberlake, Michael, 32, 39, 56
Tomlin, Brian, 8, 33, 39, 45, 48, 51-52, 55, 57, 62
trade,
and aid. *See* aid
and area. *See* area
and colonialism, 12
and consumption, 62
and debt. *See* debt
and dependencey. *See* dependency
and energy independence. *See* energy independence
and GNP. *See* GNP
and GNP per capita. *See* GNP per capita
and GNP per capita growth. *See* GNP per capita growth
and inequality. *See* inequality
and PQLI. *See* PQLI
and primary exports. *See* primary exports
and Quality Improvement. *See* Quality Improvement
and regime type. *See* regime type
as a control variable, 62
terms of, 13, 49
trade balance, 24
trade diversification, 112
trade linkages, 48
trade partner concentration, 35
and aid. *See* aid
and area. *See* area

and colonialism, 12
and consumption, 62
and debt. *See* debt
and dependencey. *See* dependency
and energy independence. *See* energy independence
and GNP. *See* GNP
and GNP per capita. *See* GNP per capita
and GNP per capita growth. *See* GNP per capita growth
and inequality. *See* inequality
and PQLI. *See* PQLI
and primary exports. *See* primary exports
and Quality Improvement. *See* Quality Improvement
and regime type. *See* regime type
as a control variable, 62
trade sanctions, 48
trade volume, 44
trade with core, 48, 95
and aid. *See* aid
and area. *See* area
and colonialism, 12
and consumption, 62
and debt. *See* debt
and dependency. *See* dependency
and energy independence. *See* energy independence
and GNP. *See* GNP
and GNP per capita. *See* GNP per capita
and GNP per capita growth. *See* GNP per capita growth
and inequality. *See* inequality
and PQLI. *See* PQLI
and primary exports. *See* primary exports
and Quality Improvement. *See* Quality Improvement
and regime type. *See* regime type
as a control variable, 62
trade with periphery, 48
traditional societies, 10.
triple alliance, 22
trade dependency, 37
t-statistic, 107
Tyler, William, 36-37

underdevelopment, 15
    definition of, 2
undeveloped, 15-16
unequal exchange, 12, 15, 22, 37
United Nations Conference on Trade
    and Development (UNCTAD), 13-
    14.
United Nations Economic Commission
    for Latin America (ECLA), 12-14.
varimax rotation, 72
Verba, Sydney, 10
wealth, *See* GNP per capita

Webster, Thomas, 33-34
weighted least squares analog, 65-66
West, Robert, 72
Williams, Bruce, 51
Wimberly, Dale, 52
Wogart, Peter, 36-37
World Bank, 48-49, 57-58, 65, 71, 103,
    109
World Intellectual Property
    Organization, 53
Young, Frank, 60

About the Author

Brian Farmer is Associate Professor of Political Science at Lubbock Christian University in Lubbock, TX. Dr. Farmer received his PH.D. in political science from Texas Tech University with an emphasis in comparative politics and an area of research specializing in the political economies of lesser developed countries. Dr. Farmer also holds an M.A. in political science from Texas Tech with a research specialization in international political economy. Dr. Farmer has been the recipient of numerous writing awards including an award for best paper at the 1994 Rocky Mountain Conference on Latin American Studies. Other writing projects include *American Public Policy* (forthcoming) from International Thompson Publishers.